Drifting, Trawling
Shipping
by
Malcolm White

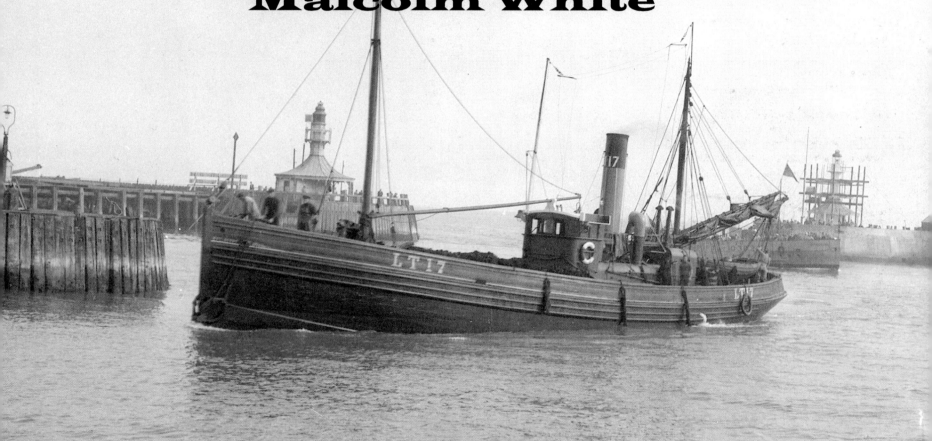

Coastal and Maritime Heritage Series

2001

INFORMATION

Published by   Malcolm R. White
71 Beeching Drive
Lowestoft
Suffolk
NR32 4TB
England
United Kingdom

Printed by   Micropress Printers Ltd
27 Norwich Road
Halesworth
Suffolk
IP19 8BX
England
United Kingdom

First Published June 2001
Copyright   ©   Malcolm R. White 2001

ISBN 0 9532485 4 2
All rights reserved

Please Note
Every effort has been made to ensure the information in this book is accurate. For this reason, official documentation backed up by various research works, and local records have been consulted for factual support. However, when considering such a complex, variable and historical subject, with some material attributable to other parties, 100% accuracy cannot be guaranteed.

Front Cover Photograph
LT557 Suffolk Crusader, one of the batch of Appledore built side trawlers, approaches the pier heads in the late 1960s.

Title page Photograph
A superb 1930s scene with the 1913 built drifter *LT17 Boy Scout* arriving home from the fishing grounds.
A pleasure steamer follows her into port.

Opposite Page Photograph
After becoming involved in offshore oil and gas support work the company had a number of specialised vessels built.
One of these was the *Suffolk Princess,* seen here on her first visit to Great Yarmouth in 1983.

CONTENTS

ACKNOWLEDGEMENTS

Many sources of information have been consulted to enable this review and comprehensive fleet list to be prepared. These include personal accounts of events, official documentation, research works, projects, and the archives of the Port of Lowestoft Research Society .

My grateful thanks to Skipper Richard Fiske and Skipper "Roly" Reynolds, both former Small & Co. skippers, for assistance during the preparation of this publication. Also, to Peter Bird of Small & Co. (Shipping) Ltd., Paul Kirby of Small & Co. (Marine Engineering) Ltd. for kindly supplying information regarding the history of their companies, and Timothy Spurrier, former Chairman of Small & Co. (Lowestoft) Ltd. for information about the Company and their ships.

Amongst the research works consulted, was that undertaken by Linda O' Carroll in 1991, with support form Louise Clarke, into the Spashett family history. As with other books in this series, the two principal societies dedicated to preserving and recording the fishing and general maritime heritage of Lowestoft and the surrounding area have been of assistance. These societies are the PLRS, and its sister society, the Lowestoft & East Suffolk Maritime Society (LESMS). The PLRS aims to compile both a written and photographic record of the vessels and industries connected in any way with the Port of Lowestoft. The LESMS is responsible for the Lowestoft & East Suffolk Maritime Heritage Museum, which is located in the Sparrows Nest, Lowestoft. Much appreciated has been the input by Hans Boje, Stanley Earl, Peter Killby, PLRS Chairman Alan Page, and my fellow officers and the members of the Society, LESMS Chairman Peter Parker, Parry Watson and David White. I am grateful to John Wells for specialised support in the presentation of historic and rare photographs in this book and also access to the John Wells Heritage Collection.

For editorial support in this series, I am very much indebted to Stuart Jones BA formerly of CEFAS Laboratory, Lowestoft.

PHOTOGRAPHIC OWNERSHIP AND COPYRIGHT

Other books in the Coastal and Maritime Series by Malcolm White.........

DOWN THE HARBOUR 1955-1995

40 years of fishing vessels, owners, the harbour and shipyards at Lowestoft   ISBN 09532485 0 X

A CENTURY OF FISHING

Fishing from Great Yarmouth and Lowestoft   ISBN 09532485 1 8

FISHING WITH DIVERSITY

A portrait of the Colne Group of Lowestoft   ISBN 09532485 2 6

CROWNIES OF LOWESTOFT

The steam trawler fleet of Consolidated Fisheries   ISBN 09532485 3 4

Web Site: www.MaritimeLowestoft.co.uk   E-mail: Books@MaritimeLowestoft.co.uk

Built at Woolwich, the stern trawler *LT171 Suffolk Warrior* remains in service as the standby safety vessel *Britannia Warrior*. She was the second vessel in the Small & Co. fleet to carry that name and is seen here off north Lowestoft in 1973 shortly after delivery.

A typical Waveney Dock scene in the 1950s during the home fishing. This superb image captured by Mr. John Wells shows at least three of the Small & Co. drifter/trawler fleet, *LT137 Norfolk Yeoman*, *LT238 Swiftwing* and *LT387 Young Duke*. Another view taken from the same location, but recorded many years later, can be seen in part two of the Photographic Review

Introduction

The name of **Small & Co.** has been associated with Lowestoft for over **150 years,** and was well known in the British fishing industry for almost 100 years. During that period, the town and surrounding area witnessed major expansion, with the Company for the majority of that time being very much at the forefront of that expansion. The principal driving forces behind the company have been Captain T. Small, the Spashett family, originating from Barking, and later the Cartwright family.

During the 150 years, the impact made upon the prosperity and business life of the area by the Company has been enormous. For a great many years, Small & Co. had a substantial presence in Great Yarmouth. For an unknown reason, this contribution to the local economy and also the British fishing industry, has not attracted the level of attention that it rightly deserves. In the 19th and 20th centuries, Small & Co. was very much a primer mover and led the fishing and local business community with a very diverse business portfolio.

A substantial part of the business of Captain Small and the Company was related to sea going activities. In the early part of the 20th century, many owners of fishing vessels had dealings with Small & Co. The majority of these vessels later became incorporated within the Company. As the years pass, it is becoming difficult to ascertain exactly what proportion of shares in vessels were owned by the Company and their many associates. It is quite possible that a number of fishing and other vessels, with which Captain Small and later the Spashetts had financial interests in, have passed unnoticed through lack of definitive ownership details. As a major fishing vessel owner, they operated a large fleet of drifters and trawlers, the Company being noted for the quality and standard of the new build vessels in their fleet. The total number of drifters owned by Small & Co. was substantial, and considered to be the largest individual fleet in the British Isles and probably the world.

To determine the origin, and the formation of Small & Co. (Lowestoft) Ltd., has meant researching and investigating many early documents, relating to individuals, companies and businesses. The principals of the Company had financial connections and business associations with a great number of other companies and individuals. In many cases, prominent positions were held within those companies.

This book provides a brief history of the Company, and reviews their drifters, trawlers, and other vessels, and also some owned by individuals and companies with financial associations with the Company. The offshore oil and gas industry support vessels, operated by the last sea going element of the Company, Suffolk Marine, are included. This subsidiary was sold in 1989. Today the name lives on, with Small & Co. (Shipping) Ltd., and Small & Co. (Marine Engineering) Ltd., well established in the industrial and maritime base of the area.

As with previous works in this series, this book is intended as a specialized fishing and maritime publication, and it is assumed that the reader has an appreciation of British fishing vessels and the industry. Imperial measures continue to be used throughout. Many other photographs of fishing vessels belonging to associates of the Company, including the *Feasible, Formidable, Mary Heeley, Strathderry, Strathlossie,* and *Togo* can be found in other books in this series.

Malcolm White
Lowestoft
June 2001

SMALL & CO. (LOWESTOFT) LTD.

LOW LIGHT & BEACH LOWESTOFT 1854

During the early 1800s, a man arrived at Lowestoft who would establish a company, which would later bring large-scale investment and hundreds of jobs directly and indirectly into the town and surrounding area.

That company, Small & Co. (Lowestoft) Ltd., was to have a major presence in the fabric and business life of the town and port of Lowestoft, for the majority of the 20th century. Today in the 21st century, the company lives on through Small & Co. (Shipping) Ltd. Their main office is in the building that was the longstanding headquarters of the original company. The services offered by this company at Waveney Chambers, follow closely those offered in the early 1800s. Another company, the principal local ship repair company, Small & Co. (Marine Engineering) Ltd. has

connections with a subsidiary of the original company.

SMALL BEGINNINGS

The beginnings of this large diverse company which became Small & Co. (Lowestoft) Ltd. can be traced back to when Captain Thomas Small, a young master mariner, left the sea and started in business as a merchant and shipping broker in the town. The harbour had yet to be built, making it necessary for all merchandise and cargoes destined for the town, as well as landings by fishing boats to be made on the beach.

Off Lowestoft, there was considerable passing traffic in coastal shipping; this mainly consisted of barques, brigs, schooners and barges. Much of this traffic was plying between London, the North East ports, and Scotland. The Corton, Holme, Newcombe and Barnard Sands made the passage past the town quite difficult and

Giving Assistance.

often dangerous, with the position of the sands changing. Many vessels met with disaster, often due to masters having outdated charts, few navigational aids and limited local knowledge of the coastal waters. Longshoremen and beachmen undertook rescue and salvage work, sometimes in fog and in storm conditions off the beach using sailing yawls, or "yolls". These slender open boats, about 50ft. in length were often launched off the beach in the teeth of a gale, and then endeavoured to claw their way out to vessels in distress on the treacherous sands. The crews of these boats needed brute force, superb seamanship and intrepid courage.

Captain Small saw an opportunity to join others and offer pilotage, to supply stores and provide repair facilities to these passing vessels, and at the same time, secure a good prosperous future for himself. These services, together with his merchant and shipping broker activities, soon established him as a much sought after, and important person in the town. To board vessels off Lowestoft, the Captain hired a company of beachmen and longshoremen equipped with yawls and gigs. These were ready day and night to take him or members of his staff out to vessels, and to offer owners and masters the many services that he was able to supply. This work was often perilous with many serious injuries being incurred by Captain Small's men, with a number losing their lives. During

1852 one of the Captain's clerks, Mr. Reeve, lost his life due to drowning and in 1854, Mr. G. West was severely injured

ESTABLISHING AND EXPANDING

A group of Norwich merchants early in the 19th century, had set about promoting and financing a plan to enable a means of access to the North Sea from the City and River Yare via Oulton Broad and Lowestoft. Alderman Crisp first placed the project before the Corporation of the City of Norwich on 3rd May 1814. After much opposition to the plan from Great Yarmouth in Parliament, the somewhat delayed Norwich & Lowestoft Navigation Bill, was passed on the 28th May 1827. The contracts for the 400ft x 50ft sea lock at Lowestoft were signed on 3rd July 1827. The complete project involved improvements to the rivers at a number of places and included the building of the new cut from Reedham to Haddiscoe, and the installation of a double-gated lock at Mutford (now Oulton Broad). A new bridge was also built at Haddiscoe. This very expensive major undertaking had been brought about by quarrels between Norwich traders and merchants, and the authorities at Yarmouth concerning a number of issues. These included the harbour dues being charged at Yarmouth, for goods

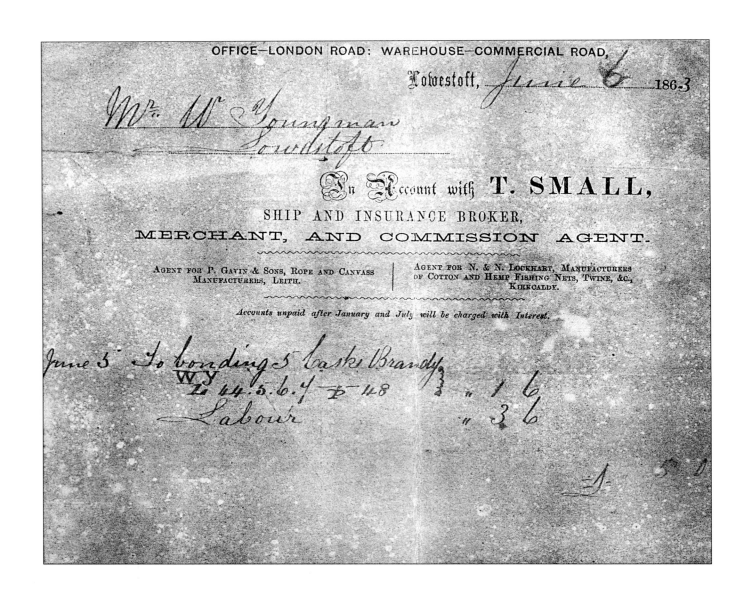

OFFICE—LONDON ROAD: WAREHOUSE—COMMERCIAL ROAD,

Lowestoft, *June 6* 186-3

Mr. W. Youngman
Lowestoft

In Account with **T. SMALL,**

SHIP AND INSURANCE BROKER,

MERCHANT, AND COMMISSION AGENT.

AGENT FOR P. GAVIN & SONS, ROPE AND CANVASS MANUFACTURERS, LEITH.

AGENT FOR N. & N. LOCKHART, MANUFACTURERS OF COTTON AND HEMP FISHING NETS, TWINE, &C., KIRKCALDY.

Accounts unpaid after January and July will be charged with Interest.

June 5   To bonding 5 Casks Brandy
WY
£ 44. 5. 6. 7 — 48   3 " 1 6
Labour   " 3 6

Copy of an original Thomas Small invoice from 1863
Courtesy of Small & Co. (Shipping) Ltd.

coming from, and going to Norwich. Generally, these were transhipped at Yarmouth. The dues charged were considered excessive, and the Norwich traders and merchants decided to set up an alternative way to the sea. Other reasons included restricted access to the harbour due to a sand bar, present under certain conditions at the harbour mouth at Gorleston, and items getting lost during the transhipping at Yarmouth.

The harbour at Lowestoft, constructed as part of this new route, opened on 10th August 1831. However for a number of years fish continued to be landed on the beach. For numerous reasons, the harbour was not as successful as had been hoped, and was closed. The harbour ownership then passed to the Public Works Loan Commissioners. In 1843, six Lowestoft businessmen purchased the harbour and undertook a number of repairs, and during 1844, the ownership passed to Mr. Morton Peto. He set about improving the harbour, and building a railway line to Reedham from Lowestoft, thereby connecting the town to Norwich, London and the rest of the country. The line opened in June 1847. The formation of the outer harbour, in use by 1848, was one of the improvements carried out under Peto and the Lowestoft Railway & Harbour Co. Ltd. From the 5th February 1845, operation and later ownership of the harbour, was the responsibility of a number of successive railway companies. The first of these operators was the Norwich & Brandon Railway, in conjunction with the Yarmouth & Norwich Railway. During this period, Captain Small with his many business ventures was becoming very well established in the town. The Captain had by now established an office at No. 1 Surrey Street. His business grew and prospered as he continued to seek out ways in which he could further expand. The amount of goods passing through Lowestoft harbour continued to increase, with the Captain well placed to take advantage of the situation.

After the construction of the North and South Piers was completed, and numerous other changes to the harbour undertaken, a substantial increase was seen in the variety of merchandise and traffic passing through the port. These included Norwegian timber, hemp from Russia, Italian oils and silks, Prussian wool, French wine, Austrian metalwork, guano from South America, Tyneside coal for industrial, maritime and domestic use, Welsh slates and Channel Island stone. A cattle trade with Denmark was set up using steam ships which was initially very successful. However, due to the transmission of animal related diseases, this venture was eventually terminated.

The growth in the numbers of vessels using the port continued. In 1873, 870 vessels entered the port; this total includes 110 steamers that had entered for trade or refuge. The port had by then become a highly important Harbour of Refuge, this having been established without any support or assistance from the Government of the day.

Lowestoft North Roads in the 1850s.

Records show it was not unusual to find 150 to 200 sailing vessel in port sheltering from storms and gales. At times, between the port and Great Yarmouth there could be as many as 700 wind bound vessels at anchor in the Roads. Indeed, more vessels were passing the east coast than any other coast in the world, and the harbour at Lowestoft was in the midst of one of the best and most frequented anchorages. However, in consequence of the many shoals and sands, the coastline could present a scene of shipwreck, devastation and death.

Captain Small, with his many talents and services was in great demand! A further expansion of his business empire saw him purchasing a number of coasting brigs. The importation of ice from Norway for the fish trade and domestic use was another trade overseen by the Captain. During 1851, he was appointed Lloyd's Agent for Lowestoft and during the next twenty years, he became vice consul for Sweden, Norway, France, Spain and Austria. Around this time he also acquired a substantial interest in various types of insurance, and held shipping agencies for Glasgow and Tyneside. In old age, the Captain continued to be an independent, shrewd, enterprising and self sufficient individual. His firm was becoming a big business, with between 780 and 1030 vessels a year entering the port of Lowestoft. He saw the need for a bonded warehouse and built one. The developments in the fishing industry at the port, created a demand for support services, including that of a rope and twine supplier. This demand was soon satisfied when the Captain set one up.

The emergence of Lowestoft as a major fishing port in the mid 1800s occurred due to several reasons, one of which was the discovery of various prolific fishing grounds in the southern North Sea. Many sailing trawlers, their owners, crews and families arrived at the ports of Lowestoft and Great Yarmouth from Barking, and various ports on the south coast. Trades people and suppliers from other ports, established in the ancillary trades, followed the fleets, and moved to the town to support the new arrivals. These included fish merchants, rope spinners, block and spar makers, sailmakers and ships chandlers. Amongst the new arrivals in the 1860s was the master blockmaker, sailmaker, shipwright and smack owner Alfred Spashett, his wife Mary, and family of five sons and four daughters. At Barking, members of the Spashett family owned a number of sailing trawlers including the *Alfred and Mary, Briton, Friends Goodwill, Royal George,*

Twins, Prosperous, and *Upton.* In addition to owning sailing trawlers, the family was well known as mast makers, net makers, shipwrights, pump makers and block makers. In addition, they were business associates of Mr. Samuel Hewett, to whom they supplied various services to maintain his famous Short Blue fleet of trawlers and cutters. On a number of occasions, Samuel Hewett made loans to the Spashett family to cover the purchase of sailing trawlers and other items of major expenditure.

In 1879, Captain Thomas Small, who had done much for the town and port of Lowestoft, and to a lesser extent Great Yarmouth, died. By then, the business was essentially shipbroking and cargo handling. The running of the business was left to the late Captain's chief clerk Mr. Wilkinson.
One of Alfred Spashett's sons, Frederick, had obtained work with Captain Small five years previous, in 1874, at the age of 13 as an apprentice office boy. Frederick soon proved to be a capable and industrious lad. Not long after the death of Captain Small, the chief clerk departed and left a note stating he was leaving the country, and the business was effectively Frederick's. From then on, the Captain's widow and executors relied largely upon Frederick, then only 18, for continuation of the business.

GROWTH AND STABILITY WITH THE SPASHETT'S

In 1881, when Frederick was twenty, he was in a position to take complete control of the company and seek ways to expand the business. Ten years later, with sustained growth in the core business, and expansion into other fields, the Company moved into new offices in Waveney Chambers, overlooking the Trawl Dock and the North Sea. It was to be these offices, later modernised, that would be home to the Company until the disposals of the assets in the 1980s and 1990s.
For a great many years, the majority of the passing trade was still carried out in sailing ships. Being reliant upon the natural elements of wind and tide, the pattern of frequent wrecks and strandings on the numerous sands and shoals, so familiar to Captain Small, continued. It was not unusual for Frederick Spashett himself, to conducted salvage attempts. The expertise and skill with which he carried out these tasks, was such that the appointment of Lloyds agent, held for many years for Lowestoft, was extended to cover the whole of the Suffolk coast. Considerable growth had been

achieved in the insurance side of the business by the end of the 19th century. Associations with many of the major insurance companies were established to provide not only cover for fishing and shipping, but also general marine, commercial, domestic and civil insurance.

Frederick married Henrietta Emma in 1882. She proved to be a truly wonderful wife, and also a great partner in his business and social relationships. Her support meant a great deal to Frederick in his work and business ambitions. Frederick and Henrietta had eight children, six daughters and two sons. Of these children, one of the daughters, Ethel Mary and one of the sons, George Frederick, stand out in relation to the continued growth and prosperity of Small & Co., Ethel was born in 1886 and George in 1884, both at the family home at Mutford near Lowestoft. George was to play a major part in the development of Small & Co., with his father in later years. Ethel married Harold Cartwright in 1911 at Mutford, and was the mother of David Frederick Cartwright. Later, he would become Major D. F. Cartwright MC, MBE, TD and the managing director of Small & Co. (Lowestoft) Ltd. Major Cartwright was often referred to as Tony, by those closest to him.

The emergence of Small & Co. as a major fishing company commenced around the end of the 19th century, when Frederick Spashett acquired a direct interest in the local fishing industry, by becoming the owner of a number of Lowestoft sailing trawlers. He was later involved in the ownership of a very large fleet of steam herring drifters, and by the 1920s, a number of large steam trawlers. Frederick was assisted in this new venture by his son George and Mr. Harry Craske, who both joined the Company in 1903. The autumn East Anglian herring fishery or "hoom fishing" as it was referred to locally, reached its peak just before the First World War. At that time, well over a thousand herring drifters, some sailing but mostly steam powered, could be found at the East Anglian ports of Lowestoft and Yarmouth. The majority of these were Scottish vessels. In 1913, out of a total of 1683 drifters, 1163 were Scottish. The Scottish drifters were accompanied by an army of support workers, many of them the famous "fisher girls", responsible for gutting and packing herring.
Herring packed in barrels became a major export cargo for shipping agents Small & Co., as great steamers arrived from many eastern European counties to take hundreds of barrels away from

Lowestoft. The "hoom fishing" was important to the Company in another way, that of owning and having financial interests in a fleet of drifters through Frederick and George Spashett. Details of some of these vessels and the many companies, with which they were involved, are described later. The period just before the First World War was very busy for Small & Co., the Spashett's, the town and port.

CHALLENGING TIMES

During the war virtually all shipping and fishing ceased, and the port became home to various naval vessels. Lowestoft drifters and trawlers, and their crews, left the port to carry out various naval duties, including minesweeping. Many vessels and their crews never returned.

During this period, Frederick was as busy as usual. He was elected Mayor of Lowestoft in 1916, and served the town in that capacity until the war ended in 1918. The German Navy contributed greatly to the overall damage that Lowestoft sustained when they bombarded the town. George Spashett went into the Army during the war and returned home having been awarded the MC, and with the rank of major. He then rejoined his father as junior partner in the Company. After the war the task of rebuilding the fleet and replacing those vessels that had been lost whilst undertaking naval service, together with reviving the fortunes of Small & Co. commenced in earnest.

Unfortunately, the herring fishing so plentiful before 1914, was never to fully revive, and it seems that the rundown of this fishery and the eventual total collapse of it, witnessed in the 1960s, may have started around this time. The formation of the County Fishing Co. Ltd. in partnership with members of the Lucas family in 1908, and the acquisition of a controlling interest in Hobson's, during 1910 had further strengthened the Spashett and Small & Co. influence in the Lowestoft fishing industry. Hobson's was a large firm of fish salesmen, merchants, auctioneers and distributors, founded in 1881. It was totally absorbed into Small & Co. in 1933. This is just one example of a company, of which there would be many more, that eventually became a totally owned part of the Small & Co. and Spashett empire. After the First World War, the Spashett's continued to be heavily involved in many business deals. A small selection of these follows : -

Steam Drifters Stores Co. Ltd.

This supplier was referred to by many as the "Emporium". Set up in 1910, the Company expanded greatly after the War and became a noted major organisation in Lowestoft, and had a branch at Padstow. It supplied a vast range of services, trades and products. These included warehousemen, rope and twine manufacturers, spinners, forwarding and railway agents, founders, refrigerating storekeepers, blacksmiths, lamp manufacturer, shipwrights, engine and steam capstan suppliers and fitters, ship repairers and carpenters, tanners, sailmakers, mast and block makers, ship chandlers, livery stable owners, coach, cart and cab suppliers, butchers, grocers and provision dealers. All fuel supplies, including the best quality British steaming coals, were also available. The Company was a major supplier to the visiting Scottish fleets as well as the local fleets. There were ten directors, all heavily involved with the fishing industry, with many being the owners of drifter and trawlers. The ten were George Catchpole, Arthur Gouldby, W. T. Tripp, Arthur and John Mitchell, Charles and Robert Harvey, Frederick Chapman, Charles Harrington, and Frederick Spashett. Company secretary was George F. Spashett, and the registered office was Waveney Chambers.

Lothian Trawlers Ltd.

Set up in 1920 to initially acquire and run as a going concern the Scottish steam trawler *A57 Pointer*. Frederick was one of four directors, the others being John Sutherland Black, James Black Cameron, and James Alexander Black. The steel hulled trawler was relatively modern, having been built in 1906 at Aberdeen.

Jack Breach Ltd.

Formed in April 1919, the company was set up to acquire the assets of J. V. Breach. The chairman was Frederick and the other directors were W. Webster, George F. Spashett, G. Bullimore and W. Dewing. A fleet of nine drifters and their gear was purchased for £51,638. Further meetings were held in 1919 and 1920, as a result of which it was decided that five more Breach vessels would be purchased, including two large steam trawlers. In 1946, the name of the company was changed to Shoals Fishing Co. Ltd., after becoming a subsidiary of Small & Co. (Lowestoft) Ltd.

Nathaniel Haycock Catchpole Ltd.

Formed in 1919, with Frederick as the chairman. It was set up to continue the business of fish merchants, originally established in 1866 by Harry and Reginald Catchpole. The company ceased trading in 1927.

N. H. CATCHPOLE, JUN.,

Fish Salesman (Ecoreur),

7, HERRING & MACKEREL MARKET,

LOWESTOFT.

CONSUL FOR BELGIUM.

Telephone 183.   Telegrams— Catchpole, Fish Salesman.

Vigilant Fishing Co. Ltd.

Founded in 1921, with George as managing director. Two of the directors were also directors of the Wilmington Fishing Co. Ltd., and Hobson's managed their drifter *Wilmington*. In 1946, Major Cartwright became managing director, with the company being wound up in 1962.

Resolute Fishing Co. Ltd.

Formed in 1919 with Frederick as the chairman and George as secretary and shareholder. It was the owner of four large former Aberdeen steam trawlers, and numerous drifters. Frederick later became sole owner of the company.

In 1926, he sold it to the Grassholme Syndicate. This had been formed with 14 members to take over the assets of the Company from Frederick. In 1933, the assets of the syndicate were transferred to Small & Co. (Lowestoft) Ltd.

Cooperative Ships Stores Ltd.

Founded in 1920 by a syndicate headed by Frederick and George. Initially traded as netmakers, riggers and tinsmiths, and later expanded into being suppliers of many other types of merchandise. Wound up in 1949 after being totally acquired by Small & Co. (Lowestoft) Ltd.

Duncan Skinner Ltd.

This firm of fish curers was founded in 1920, with Frederick as a director. Ceased trading in 1926, when the assets of the company were acquired by Small & Co. (Lowestoft) Ltd.

The period between the wars saw the Spashetts considerably increasing the number of companies which were either under their control, or where their influence was strongly felt. In many businesses, there were several partners, and later these were bought out, thus obtaining 100% ownership. In 1922, the Company purchased a defunct shipyard, believed to be that owned by Colby Bros. This was later sold on to Alliance Artificial Silk. Many other companies such as the Export Fish Company, London Spinning Co. (Lowestoft) Ltd., and Waddingtons (Fuel) Ltd., had their registered offices at Waveney Chambers. The Lowestoft Fishing Vessels Owners Association, founded in 1919 with George as the Company Secretary also had its registered office there. Frederick and George became leading figures in the civic and commercial life of Lowestoft. Both held extensive interests in the fishing industry, and were directors of a vast number of East Anglian companies. During 1931, Frederick was honoured with the insignia of the Order of St. Olav, in recognition of 25 years of service to Norway as vice consul. For a man who started his working life as an office boy, his many achievements were truly impressive. He always gave the impression of a person born to lead, and was never afraid of hard work and difficult decisions.

DIFFICULT TIMES

The period between the wars saw two depressions in 1921 and 1931; these seriously affected the fishing industry and the Port of Lowestoft. The Second World War in 1939 started with the Company and the family's fortunes at a very low ebb. Fishing clients owed the company at least at £150,000. Hobsons sold the fish landed by their drifters and trawlers on commission and a number of their clients had financial problems. The Company survived by seeking support from the bank. This was forthcoming, but only after Frederick had provided a personal guarantee. During the late 1930s, George Spashett discussed the possible sale of the business to the General Steam Navigation Co. Ltd., and in fact did sell the Great Yarmouth branch of Small & Co. Ltd.

For the town, the port, and Small & Co., the Second World War saw the pattern of the previous war repeated, with drifters and trawlers again requisitioned for naval service, and the use of the port severely restricted and given over to military operations. Throughout the war, the town suffered a great many air attacks, with substantial damage occurring over a wide area. However, on the 13th January 1943, the town found time to present the Honorary Freedom of the Borough to Frederick Spashett at the Town Hall. This great occasion was followed in the autumn of that year, by the devastating news of the death of his son George. The tremendous blow was described in the local press as "Lowestoft's Great Loss". The Mayor in the Council Chamber described George as "one of the most outstanding men of the town, and what he has done for Lowestoft it is impossible to emulate". George died at Lincoln in hospital following an operation. He was a member of the Town Council and an alderman. A few years before the war he had been appointed a Justice of the Peace and in 1939 was deputy mayor, with many looking forward to the day when he would be mayor. George repeatedly declined the offer due to work commitments. He was held in high esteem for his superb business qualities and his caring and charming nature. In spite of pressure of work, he accepted the position of Chief Warden and sub controller of Air Raid Precautions for the town. Hundreds of people respected him for his genuinely sympathetic understanding and help, given to many over the years and during the war. He took a keen interest in the social and recreational life of the town especially Oulton Broad, were he was involved with the British Legion and the swimming and sailing clubs.

THE NEW ERA

Cessation of hostilities in 1945 saw Lowestoft depressed and in need of much rebuilding, after the heavy bombing it had received. Major David Frederick Cartwright joined the family business in 1945 after serving with distinction in the Norfolk Yeomanry during the war. His military service earned him the MC, MBE and the TD. Upon joining Small & Co., he set to learning all he could about the business from Frederick. Unfortunately, only nine months after Major Cartwright joined Small & Co., Frederick died at the age of 88. In old age, he had become almost blind, but remained active in the company. At the end of the war Small & Co. was just ticking over with a staff of six people; the firm had virtually been in hibernation during the war years with little business. What work there was consisted of collecting the charter money from the Admiralty, undertaking some work the Admiralty passed out to the Company, and looking after the *Boys Friend* and *Trier*, which were fishing from Fleetwood. All other vessels in the fleet of drifters and trawlers had been requisitioned for war service. The first priority after the war was to get the vessels back from Admiralty service and to rebuild the fleet. With over 60 owned or managed fishing vessels in the fleet before the war, less than eighteen came back.

Those that did were in a bad condition, and needed much money spent on them. Some were getting on in years, and were life expired. The financial ownership arrangements of a number of these vessels meant that whilst Small & Co. did not own them outright, their owners owed the Company large sums of money, thereby giving the Company considerable influence over the vessels.

LEADERSHIP

A tremendous challenge faced Major Cartwright, and he set about sorting out the best of the vessels and returning them to fishing, in some cases acquiring the owning company's or individual's interests in the process. By this means and acquiring others, he was able to build up a fleet of around 25 vessels by 1949. Many owners were getting on in years, and were glad to get out of fishing and ship ownership. All of the vessels were steam powered, and whilst a number were steel hulled, many were of wooden construction. One problem facing Small & Co. and the fishing industry in the late 1940s was the need for high quality and speedy distribution of the large amount of fish being landed by the expanding trawler fleet. As a way to overcome this problem, Small & Co established Explorator Ltd., a well known drifter owner, in 1947 as a fish distribution concern. With over fifty vehicles on the road, the company under managing director Mr. S. Stevens, rapidly became a national leader in the fish distribution business. This company was sold in 1964 to the Ross Group, but remained in the town for many years under their ownership.

Small & Co., under Major Cartwright, set about disposing of the steam powered vessels, and introduced a new building programme for their fleet in 1949, when the first of many, the *Frederick Spashett* was delivered. Building of the first new diesel powered drifter/trawlers involved borrowing £120,000 from the bank. Many well-known vessels came into service during the next few years including *Young Elizabeth* and *Young Duke* (introduced in 1953 Coronation year), *George Spashett* (the grandfather of Major Cartwright), *Ethel Mary* and *Harold Cartwright* (the mother and father of Major Cartwright) and *Norfolk Yeoman* (the Major's unit was the Norfolk Yeomanry during the war). All of these vessels displayed the Small & Co. houseflag, which was blue with a white "S" between two white lines. The last drifter/trawler, the *Suffolk Warrior* was launched in 1960, but the new build policy for trawlers continued until 1980. A number of the drifters went on to win the famous "Prunier Trophy" for herring catching. As managing director of the subsidiary East Anglian Ice & Cold Storage Co. Ltd., Major Cartwright ordered for that long established owner, the *W.F. Cockrell* and *B. R. Banks.* Others would follow, all carrying the emblem of a cockerel just below the funnel. Richards shipyard at Lowestoft carried out the majority of this new building, completing over 20 vessels for the Company and their associates. This included both vessels named *Suffolk Mariner,* the second of which was a supply vessel, completed in 1986. A small number of previously owned, relatively modern vessels were purchased, the most notable of these being the fleet of six "Ocean" drifter/trawlers in 1963. These vessels had been built by Richards between 1952 and 1957 for the Great Yarmouth owner Bloomfields Ltd. All six were to retain their original names, but their Yarmouth fishing registrations were replaced by those of

Lowestoft. Amongst other purchases were a number of Grimsby trawlers.

The herring fishery, for so many years the main stay of the Lowestoft fishing industry, had continued to decline and in April 1966, it was disclosed that Small & Co. were phasing out herring catching and if any acceptable offers were received for their drifters, they would be sold. The last two Small & Co. drifters, the *Norfolk Yeoman* and *Ocean Surf* finished herring fishing in 1967. The reasons for the virtual wipe-out of the herring shoals are well documented, with over-fishing and industrial fishing by eastern European countries thought to a major cause for their disappearance. By this time in the mid 1960s, Lowestoft had gained the reputation of the premier near water trawling port in the UK, and the Company had become well established as an operator of a large fleet of superb modern trawlers. Initially these were side fishing vessels, later to be joined by stern trawlers. After completion in 1980 of their stern trawler *Suffolk Champion*, the only vessels built for Small & Co. were for offshore oil and gas support work. The Company having become involved in this work at about the same time as their withdrawal from herring catching.

DIVERSIFICATION

One of early activities of the firm, that of insurance, came under review in 1965. During that year, the department dealing with this was made into a separate limited company, Small & Co. (Insurance) Ltd. As a result of negotiations in 1966 with leading Lloyds broker Bray, Gibb & Co., a new company was formed, Bray, Gibb (East Anglia) Ltd. with offices in Waveney Chambers. Small & Co. (Insurance) Ltd. then became a subsidiary of the new company. Bray, Gibb & Co. had at that time a network of branches throughout the UK, and a number overseas. Mr. R. G. Cartwright, managing director of Small & Co. (Insurance) Ltd. became managing director of the new company, and retained his position on the main board of Small & Co. (Lowestoft) Ltd. In addition to the events already mentioned, during the 35 years, that Major Cartwright managed Small & Co., the offices were extended and modernised and a number of major acquisitions took place. These included the coal and fuel business Craske Ltd., the printers Flood & Son Ltd., and the marine and general engineers William Overy Ltd. In 1963, Craske Ltd. was substantially expanded, and Craske (Petroleum) Ltd. formed to distribute to the trade, and to shipping at ports between Humberside and the Thames. The main Ford car dealer Days Garage Ltd. was acquired in 1964. Others included Waveney Finance Ltd., Lowestoft Ice Co. Ltd., Gorleston Coaling Co. Ltd., Modern Heating Services, Lowestoft Coaling Co. Ltd., Oulton Broad Service Station and Great Yarmouth Service Station. March 1967, saw the Company purchase a tyre dealer, Anglian KenTred Ltd. Perhaps the most unusual business venture by the Company during this period, was the purchase of Churchgate Manor at Old Harlow and Sprowston Manor near Norwich. Both of these establishments were high quality hotels. In addition to Major Cartwright's duties with Small & Co., he was for many years the Managing Director of the East Anglian Ice & Cold Storage Co. Ltd. This company was later disposed of to the Lowestoft Fishing Vessel Owners Association.

During 1959, marine engineers William Overy & Son set up at Loddon, the Broads holiday cruiser hire firm Princess Cruisers Ltd. They built many cruisers for the new company between 1959 and 1963, these boats being allocated names such as *Coral Princess, Gipsy Princess, Golden Princess, Lister Princess, Radiant Princess* and *Summer Princess*. When William Overy became part of the Small Group, Princess Cruisers Ltd. was included in the acquisition. In December 1967, Aston Boats Ltd. of Loddon acquired this Small Group subsidiary and the fleet of cruisers. Once in Aston ownership these cruisers were all renamed.

RATIONALISATION AND DISPOSAL

With ever-increasing fuel and general running costs, the depressed state of the industry and increasing legislation, trawler ownership by Small & Co. ended in May 1984 when their newest and last trawler, the *Suffolk Champion*, was withdrawn from fishing. Following the cessation of fishing, the sea going activities of the Company consisted of support work for the offshore oil and gas industries. Initially many of the vessels used on this work were their redundant drifters and trawlers. These were soon replaced by more suitable vessels, some of which were new build. A new subsidiary company, Suffolk Marine, was later formed to focus on the booming offshore support market. This Company was sold in 1989, together with the very modern fleet of vessels to local operator Britannia Marine. The Suffolk Marine fleet acquired by Britannia comprised five standby safety vessels, two anchor

handling/supply vessels and one supply ship. Following the sale, the Suffolk Marine organisation was integrated with that of the new owning Company, which was based in Columbus Buildings in Waveney Road, Lowestoft. After the spring of 1989, the well-known blue flag with a white "S" between two white lines no longer belonged to the Small & Co. group and disappeared from Waveney Chambers. However, for several months it could still be seen on vessels of the former Suffolk fleet, even after their new owner had renamed them. Eventually, the head of Britannia replaced the flag of Small & Co. on these vessels. The sea going activities of this once great company had finally come to an end.

The last Chairman of Small & Co. (Lowestoft) Ltd. was Mr. Timothy Spurrier, whose mother, Barbara, was a daughter of George Spashett. At one time, the company had well over 700 employees, and brought wealth and prosperity to the town. The associated companies could be found operating in many different sections of the local economy, creating employment and providing investment. Local shipbuilders were kept busy with the large number of vessels ordered by the Company. Over the years, the policy of progressive development across a wide spectrum of trades and services, did much to further the industrial development of Lowestoft. Disposal of the many assets of Small & Co. (Lowestoft) Ltd. continued over a number of years. Waveney Chambers, for over 80 years the head office of the original company, now hosts the offices of a number of different organisations. One of these is Eastern Counties Newspapers, whose local offices can be found there. This company publishes the weekly newspaper, "Lowestoft Journal" and the daily newspaper "Eastern Daily Press".

Today at the start of the 21st century, Small & Co. (Shipping) Ltd. maintains the famous Small name and presence in Waveney Chambers. Part of the original company, it was the subject of a management buyout in 1996. The company has held the Lloyds agency continuously since 1892 and the position of Norwegian consul for Norfolk and Suffolk since the mid 1850s. Small & Co. (Shipping) Ltd. is a member of the British International Freight Association, and Institute of Chartered Shipbrokers.

With Managing Director, Mr. Peter Bird, the company prides itself on their professionalism and commitment to meeting the specific requirements of each individual customer, something that in the early 19th century, Captain Thomas Small set out to achieve.

A selection of Small group and Spashett subsidiary companies, business associates, syndicates and partnerships :-

Admiral Fishing Co. Ltd. - Fishing Vessel Owner
Allerton C. G. - Fishing Vessel Owner
Anglian Ken-Tred Ltd - Tyre Distributors
Beck E. - Fishing Vessel Owner
Black Cat Fishing Co. Ltd. - Fishing Vessel Owner
Bond. H - Fishing Vessel Owner
Boy Alan Ltd. - Fishing Vessel Owner
Bray, Gibb (East Anglia) Ltd. - Insurance
Breach J. V. - Fishing Vessel Owner
Britannia Fishing Co. Ltd. - Fishing Vessel Owner
Bullimore G. H. - Fishing Vessel Owner
E. T. Capps & Sons Ltd.- Fishing Vessel Owner/ Merchants
Capps, Frederick G. - Fish Salesman
Contract Hire (Days) Ltd. - Car and Van Hire
Colonial Fishing Co. Ltd. - Fishing Vessel Owner
Cooperative Ships Stores Ltd. - Shipping Supplier
County Fishing Co. Ltd. - Fishing Vessel Owner
Craske (Petroleum) Ltd. - Fuel Merchants and Distributors
Craske Ltd. - Fuel Merchants and Distributors
Dance, Charles - Fish Salesman/ Owner
Days Garage Ltd. - Ford Main Dealers
Drifting & Trawling Total Loss Mutual Insurance Co. Ltd. - Insurance
Duncan Skinner Ltd. - Fish Merchants and Curers
Eastern Drifters Ltd. - Fishing Vessel Owner
C. V. Eastick Ltd. - Fishing Vessel Owner
East Anglian Ice & Cold Storage Co. Ltd. - Vessel Owner/ Ice Supplier
East Anglian Red Star Fishing Co. Ltd. - Fishing Vessel Owner
Explorator Ltd. - Fishing Vessel Owner/ Fish Processing and Distribution
Export Fish Co. Ltd.- Fish Exporters, Merchants and Packers
Flood & Son Ltd. - Printers
Fowlers (Beccles) Ltd. - Fuel Merchants and Distributors
Gorleston Coaling Co. Ltd. - Fuel Merchants and Distributors
Grassholme Syndicate - Fishing Vessel Owner
Great Yarmouth Shipping Co. Ltd. - Cargo Ship Owners
Hayward J. C. - Fishing Vessel Owner
Hobson & Co. Ltd. - Fishing Vessel Owner/ Fish Sales
Hobson (Lowestoft) Ltd. - Fishing Vessel Owner/Fish Sales
E. R. Ives Ltd - Transport Contractors
Jack Breach Ltd. - Vessel Owner
Kittiwake Ltd. - Fishing Vessel Owner
London Spinning Co. (Lowestoft) Ltd.– Net and Fabric Manufactures
Lothian Trawlers Ltd. - Trawler owners
Lowestoft Coaling Co. Ltd. - Fuel Merchants and Distributors

Lowestoft Drift Fishing Vessel Total Loss Mutual Insurance - Insurance
Lowestoft Fishing Vessel Owners Association - Owners Association
Lowestoft Ice Company - Ice Importers, Manufacturers and Suppliers
Lowestoft Marine Engine & Boiler Insurance Association-Insurance
Lowestoft Mutual Fishing Vessel Insurance Society - Insurance
Lowestoft Trawler United Insurance Association Ltd. - Insurance
Lowestoft Water & Gas Co. Ltd. - Utility Services Provider
Modern Heating Services (East Anglia) Ltd. - Heating Specialists
D. W. Motors (Lowestoft) Ltd. - Motor Engineers
Nathaniel Haycock Catchpole Ltd. - Fish Curer and Merchant
Oulton Broad Advancement Association - Area Promotion
Oulton Broad Service Station - Garage, Fuel Services and Vehicle Sales
Outlaw T. - Fishing Vessel Owner
Percy Wigg Ltd. – Fuel, Engineers, Haulage, Coach and Cab owners
Pevensey Castle Ltd. - Fishing Vessel Owner
Princess Cruisers Ltd. - Broads Holiday Cruiser Owner/ Letting
Ploughboy Co. Ltd. - Fishing Vessel Owner
Resolute Fishing Co. Ltd. - Fishing Vessel Owner
Rivett R. - Fishing Vessel Owner
Seagull Fishing Co. Ltd. - Fishing Vessel Owner
Seagull Manufacturing Co. Ltd. - Metal Fabricators
Self Drive (Lowestoft) Ltd. - Car and Van Hire
Service Station (Gt. Yarmouth) Ltd. - Garage, Fuel Services and Vehicle Hire
Shoals Fishing Co. Ltd. - Fishing Vessel Owner
Small & Co. (Insurance) Ltd. - Insurance
Small & Co. (Lowestoft) Ltd. - Corporate Organisation/Vessel Owners
Small & Co. (Marine Engineering) Ltd - Marine and General Engineers
Small & Co. (Shipping) Ltd. - Shipping Agents
T. Small & Co. Ltd. - Shipping Agents (Great Yarmouth)
Smith H. E. - Fishing Vessel Owner
Southwold Service Station - Garage and Fuel Services
Spashett & Co. Ltd.- Retailers of Stationary, Books, Fancy Goods, Wools
Spashett Frederick - Vessel Owner/Company Principal / Mayor
Spashett George F. - Vessel Owner/ Company Principal/ Alderman
Steam Drifters Stores Co. Ltd. - Ship Supplier, Fitters, Blacksmiths
Suffolk Marine Ltd. - Supply and Safety Vessel Owners
Trier Fishing Co. Ltd. - Fishing Vessel Owner
Utting T. A. - Fishing Vessel Owner
Vectis Steam Fishing Co. Ltd. - Trawler Owners, Fish Merchants
Victory Fishing Co. Ltd. - Fishing Vessel Owner
Vigilant Fishing Co. Ltd. - Fishing Vessel Owner
Waveney Finance Co. Ltd. - Financial and Insurance Services
White Star Fishing Co. Ltd. - Fishing Vessel Owner
William Overy & Son Ltd. - Marine Engineers, Boat Builders and Crane Hire

Hotels

Churchgate Manor - Old Harlow   Sprowston Hall - Sprowston, Norwich

PHOTOGRAPHIC REVIEW - PART ONE

Frederick and George Spashett would recognise both these views of Lowestoft, and the scene below would have been familiar to Captain Small.

LOWESTOFT. INNER HARBOUR. (106.)

Above - The Inner Harbour just before the First World War, with the rebuilt Great Eastern Railway paddle tug *Imperial* visible on the right.

Left - The Outer Harbour, the first fish market and the yacht basin during the 1870s.

The headquarters of Small & Co. (Lowestoft) Ltd. were at Waveney Chambers in Waveney Road. The building was extensively modernised in 1967.

Above - Dating from the early 20th century, Waveney Chambers is essentially as built in this 1950s view.

Right - The building as modernised

Through their subsidiary company Explorator Ltd., Small & Co. led the way in processing, packing and national distribution of fish. These two scenes were recorded in 1963. Explorator eventually became part of the Ross Group.

Above - A scene at the western end of No. 1 Hall

Right - The fish packing station and Market Office was in Battery Green Road.

On the 6th April 1960 a party of M.P.s visited Lowestoft, and met representatives of the fishing industry.
Part of their tour was to the Explorator Market Office where Mr. S. A. Stevens of Explorator Ltd. is seen explaining the workings of the nation-wide teleprinter and telex system to Sir William Duthie.

In addition to the excellent qualities of their products, Explorator became well known for their large fleet of Thames Trader insulated vehicles. This scene was recorded at the Crisps Wharf garage and shows maintenance work being carried out on a small selection of the fleet. Due to the high mileages travelled, maintenance was of the highest standard.

On the day of the M.P.s. visit in 1960, a group of well known fishing industry representatives gather on the Herring Market. Left to right:- Mr. Stevens of Claridge Trawlers, Mr. S. A. Stevens of Explorator and two trawler owners Mr. Gordon Claridge and Mr. Frederick Catchpole.

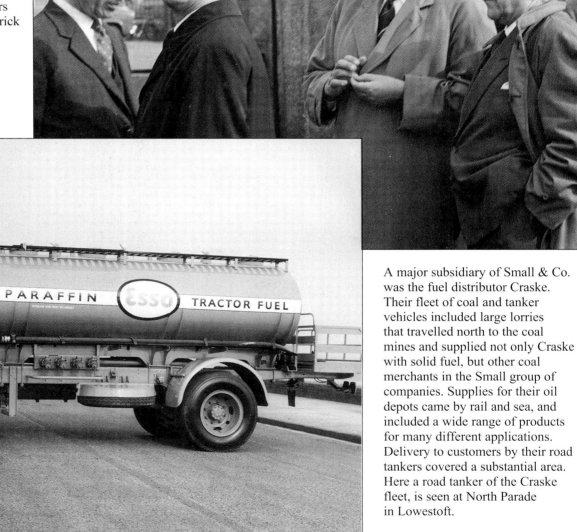

A major subsidiary of Small & Co. was the fuel distributor Craske. Their fleet of coal and tanker vehicles included large lorries that travelled north to the coal mines and supplied not only Craske with solid fuel, but other coal merchants in the Small group of companies. Supplies for their oil depots came by rail and sea, and included a wide range of products for many different applications. Delivery to customers by their road tankers covered a substantial area. Here a road tanker of the Craske fleet, is seen at North Parade in Lowestoft.

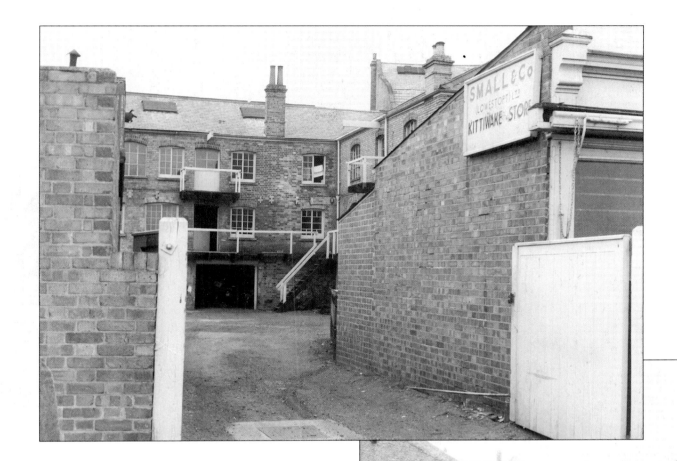

The Company had a number of net stores in Lowestoft.

Above - One of the largest was the Kittwake in the town centre. It is now the site of Marks & Spencer's car park.

Right - An example of a smaller store was Hastings House in Whapload Road, the location of many similar netstores. Many remain today serving a variety of uses.

The diverse nature of the business activities of Small & Co. are illustrated here in these examples

Above - Metal fabrication for marine, general and food processing use was carried out in the workshops of the Seagull Manufacturing Co. Ltd. in Whapload Road. William Overy & Son Ltd in Battery Green Road undertook heavy engineering, ship repair and plant hire services.

Left - Vast amounts of herring were exported from Lowestoft. This scene shows employees of the Export Fish Co Ltd. assembled for the photographer in 1902.

A classic view of the harbour entrance with the sailing trawler *LT679 Sarepta* leaving port and the steam drifter *LT289 John and Sarah* arriving from the fishing grounds. Later in life the *John and Sarah* was fitted with a wheelhouse.

Following a collision with *YH843 Ludham Castle* off Great Yarmouth in December 1911, the *John and Sarah* was beached at Gorleston and later broken up. She was built by John Chambers at Lowestoft in 1901.

This superb view shows the drifter *LT175 Nil Desperandum* in a very busy Inner Harbour at Lowestoft. Owned by Jack Breach Ltd. she was built in 1903 and sold for breaking up at Oulton Broad in 1936.

The steam drifter *LH3 Resolute* was built in 1886 at Leith. She was purchased in 1919 by Frederick Spashett and sold on during the same year. *Resolute* is seen here leaving Yarmouth harbour, prior to 1914 when in the ownership of Mr. W. Wilcox. She ended her days as a lighter at Grimsby.

The *Mary Bruce* was purchased by the Shoals Fishing Co. Ltd. in 1948 and was allocated the registration *LT368*. She was built in 1910 at Beverley and sold for scrapping in 1953. This view shows her approaching the Lowestoft piers on on 12th August 1949.

The steam drifter *LT369 Reverberation* was numerically next to *Mary Bruce* but a very different vessel. Owned by Jack Breach Ltd., this wooden hulled vessel was built in 1919 by Colby Bros. at Oulton Broad and was partially broken up in 1947. The hulk remained visible on the south shore of Lake Lothing until the early 1960s. We find her here in the mid 1930s approaching the Lowestoft harbour entrance.

The Lowestoft drifter *LT133 Strive* was built as *YH665 Fred Salmon* in 1912 by Crabtree at Great Yarmouth. She was sold and became *BK417 Ocean Plough* in 1921. By the end of 1930, *Strive* had joined the Lowestoft fleet and been allocated the registration *LT133*. She left Lowestoft in May 1953 for the shipbreakers yard.

Above - *LT133 Strive* in Scottish waters

Right   - The *Strive* earlier in her life as *BK417 Ocean Plough* leaving the harbour at Great Yarmouth

For many years Lowestoft and Yarmouth drifter/trawlers fished out of Padstow for part of the year. This scene from the 1930s shows a group of vessels which includes three, that during their lives would be associated with Smalls, the *Ploughboy*, *Herring Searcher* and *Feasible*.

The Vigilant Fishing Co. drifter *LT316 Meg* was built as *YH397* for H. J. Sayes. She joined the Lowestoft fleet in 1909. *Meg* was declared a total loss in 1936 after running ashore on the Yorkshire coast.

The crew of the drifter *LT534 Go Ahead* assembled on board for the photographer in the late 1920s. From left to right they are:- Driver Billy "Coalie" Bowles, Lenie Sturman, unknown, Bobby Johnson (with lifebelt), unknown, Skipper Jack High(in wheelhouse), unknown, Mate Henry Spencer. The Colby Bros. builders plate is prominent above the centre window. The *Go Ahead* was laid down as *HMD Volume*.

Built as *Dorothy F.* by Fellows at Great Yarmouth in 1915, the *Olivae* was sold to Caister owner Charles George and allocated the Yarmouth registration *YH73*. After a spell in Ramsgate ownership in the early 1920s, Frederick Spashett purchased her in 1924. She remained a Small & Co. drifter/trawler in the ownership of Pevensey Castle Ltd. as *LT1297* for the next 32 years, going to scrap in 1956.

During both world wars, drifters and trawlers from many fishing ports were requisitioned or chartered for naval use, including the great majority of vessels belonging to the many associated companies of Small & Co. Many vessels were lost or badly damaged, with crew members losing their lives or being severely injured.

As a tribute to the heroism and devotion to duty of crews of fishing vessels in both wars, two drifters in Admiralty service have been featured here.

The drifter *Score Head* was built as *LT1096 Retriever* in 1909. After a period in Scottish ownership as *KY34* she was purchased by Explorator Ltd. in 1930 and transferred to Pevensey Castle Ltd. the same year, when she became *LT120 Score Head*. She was sold on in 1946, and eventually sold for scrapping in 1951. *Score Head* is seen here on one of the Laundry Lane slipways with *LT711 Lord Fisher* occupying the adjacent slipway.

In 1913, a newly completed *LT199 Pevensey Castle* is seen approaching the Lowestoft harbour entrance during trials. Built by John Chambers, she was powered by a 25hp Elliott & Garrood triple expansion engine. *Pevensey Bay* had a relatively short life, and sank following a collision on 9th June 1924 .

Above Left   - The crew of the drifter/trawler *Herring Searcher* pause for the photographer. The vessel is rigged for trawling.

Above Right   - As a drifter, *LT276 Herring Searcher* heads for the pier heads. In 1949, under Skipper Stanley Turrell she won the Prunier Trophy.

Bottom Right - The drifter/trawler *LT246 Neves* leaves her home port for the fishing grounds She was later converted to diesel power and renamed *Fellowship*.

With 160 cran of herring, *LT534 Fume* arrives at Lowestoft pier heads on 14th October 1929. A "standard" drifter, she was launched as *HMD Fume* in 1919 at Colby Bros. yard in Oulton Broad. *Fume* was sold in 1930 by the Vigilant Fishing Co. Ltd. to Mauritius owners.

Originally Scottish owned with the registration *BF495*, *Three Kings* came under the Spashett influence in 1919 when purchased by Jack Breach Ltd. She was allocated the registration *LT517* and later served as a minesweeper in the Second World War. *Three Kings* was sold for scrapping in 1950.

Built for Dutch owners, the *Amalia* was purchased by Vigilant Fishing Co. Ltd. in 1930 when she received the Lowestoft registration *LT241*. *Amalia* returned to Lowestoft in 1945 after Naval service as a minesweeper and was sold to Norway the following year.

A superb shot of the drifter/trawler *LT1157 Sarah Hide*. She and her sister ship *Margaret Hide* were well known at many fishing ports around the British Isles. Fine products of Scottish shipbuilders they were both sold to Belgium for scrapping in 1955 after long and successful careers.

At one time, the funnel markings used on vessels owned by Frederick Spashett and his associates followed a pattern. This was a letter, indicating the owner, set between two lines. Many observers firmly believe that the "S" used on the houseflag stands for Spashett and not, as generally thought, Small & Co. Certainly the Spashett family were the main driving force for most of the Company's existence and therefore this may well be the case. In later years it may have been assumed that the "S" stood for Small when in fact it was a continuation of the Spashett marking. In 1911, Frederick had *LT 1134 Shipmates* built by Crabtree at Great Yarmouth. The funnel markings clearly show an "S" between two lines. Similar pattern markings were found on many vessels such as those belonging to the Admiral, Colonial and Dreadnought companies, and the Captain Lucas vessels.

Vessel passing Pier Head, Lowestoft.

A very rare early 20th century postcard showing *LT103 Norfolk County* leaving Lowestoft and rigged for trawling. Built in 1925 at Selby by Cochrane, she was sold to Norway in 1946 and converted to diesel propulsion.
In 2001, she returned to UK waters after purchase for use as a houseboat.

Left - The steam drifter *LT1059 Suffolk County* was unique in that she was the only steam "Suffolk" ever in the fleet. She was built in 1907 by Chambers at Lowestoft. *Suffolk County* is seen here at Lowestoft whilst in Scottish ownership with the fishing registration *FR30*.

Right - *LT1294 Young Dawn* was built in 1916 as *A665* for S. Herring Fleet Ltd. She was purchased in 1923 by Frederick Spashett and is seen here approaching Lowestoft pier heads on 23rd September 1927. Later that year she was sold to Peterhead and became registered as *PD178*.

Left - On the day before her maiden trip, the newly completed drifter/trawler *LT188 Tritonia* approaches the pier heads at her homeport after completion of final trials. The date of this rare and historic scene is 30th October 1930.

Above - A fine view recorded on 30th September 1930 of the steam drifter *LT68 Reunited*. Formerly Scottish owned, *Reunited* was lost on the 23rd November 1938.

Right - *LT106 Kent County* was built for County Fishing in 1929 and sold in 1932. On the 3rd Oct. 1930, she is seen off Lowestoft.

Top Left   -   An unusual venture in 1947 was the purchase and conversion into a passenger vessel of a minesweeper. She was named the *Green Dolphin* and we find her here in the bridge channel in her role as a pleasure craft.

Top Right   -   The 1953 built *LT375 Young Elizabeth*

Bottom right -   Named after Major Cartwright's mother, *LT337 Ethel Mary* heads for sea.

The trawler *LT203 Annrobin* was an early new build ordered by Major Cartwright as part of the modernisation plan. Originally in the colours of the East Anglia Ice & Cold Storage Co Ltd., we find her here in the colours of Small & Co.

LT238 Swiftwing was built as the steam-powered drifter/trawler *Sternus* in 1925 by Cochrane at Selby. Her conversion to diesel power and renaming took place in 1954. She was sold to Hartlepool owners in 1964 and scrapped in 1970. *Swiftwing* is seen entering Lowestoft on return from the herring grounds.

Above - The first of the new generation of drifter/trawlers built for Small & Co. appeared in 1949. Richards at Lowestoft were responsible for these attractive vessels. *LT138 Frederick Spashett*, seen here in Scottish waters, was the first completed.

Right - *LT295 Suffolk Maid* was the first diesel powered trawler specifically built for Small & Co., and also the first new build with a name prefixed "Suffolk".

Top Left   -   Skipper Richard Fiske in the
                wheelhouse of the drifter/
                trawler *LT82 Henrietta
                Spashett* whilst fishing out of
                Aberdeen in the mid 1950s.
Bottom Left -   *LT82 Henrietta Spashett.*
Top Right   -   A Lowestoft market scene
                from the 1960s, with herring
                being sold. Included are, from
                left to right, Reggie
                Snowling, Jim "Mucko"
                Buckingham, Bill Hingham,
                Hobson's auctioneer George
                Thoms, Barney Bemment,
                Ralph Butcher, Tich Ayers
                and George Wicks.

Built at the local shipyard of Brooke Marine in 1948, the drifter/trawler *LT343 Madame Prunier* came into the ownership of Pevensey Castle Ltd., a Small group subsidiary, in 1953. Completed for the Scottish Cooperative Wholesale Society she was powered by a 265hp Crossley engine, and built of English oak with decking of Oregon pine. In many aspects, her design was similar to the Admiralty Motor Fishing Vessels which were produced in large numbers in the 1940s. The casing of the engine room, the funnel and parts of the wheelhouse were of aluminium alloy. *Madame Prunier* was renamed *Croidte Au Duin* in 1961 and was broken up at Kilkeel in 1990. This fine view of her leaving Lowestoft for the herring grounds is by Mr. John Wells.

In addition to Major Cartwright's duties with Small & Co., he was Managing Director of the East Anglian Ice & Cold Storage Co. Ltd. for many years. The companies were closely associated and two of the East Anglian Ice & Cold Storage Ice Co. trawlers are featured here.

Above - Hauling in progress on board LT34 *Leonard Cockrell* in the mid 1960s. On the left is Third Hand W. Bridge, in the centre Mate Sam Sarbutt, and on the right a deckhand.

Left - You can almost hear the Ruston engine of *LT257 B. R. Banks* as she heads for the pier heads and sea at Lowestoft. The emblem of her owner, a red cockerel, can be clearly seen.

The drifter that caught the largest single haul of herring with one shot, in one night, during the home fishing at Lowestoft and Yarmouth was eligible for the award of the Prunier Trophy. The competition for the trophy ran from 1936 until 1966, with the exception of the war years, and 1965. The trophy was given by Madame Simone Prunier, the owner of a restaurant in London. Skippers of Small & Co. drifters were winners of the Prunier Trophy on a number of occasions. Other aspects of winning included a trip to London for the skipper and crew, and the gift of a weathervane for the top of the drifter's mizzen mast.

Above -   In 1963, Mr. Ritson Simms was Skipper of the winning drifter, *LT137 Norfolk Yeoman*. The Mayor of Lowestoft Mr.Charles Ramm is seen presenting Skipper Simms with the weathervane for the drifter. Also present are Mr. F. Catchpole and the Chairman of Small & Co., Mr. D. F. Cartwright

Right -   The winning drifter in 1961 was *LT61 Dick Whittington* under Skipper Leo Borrett. Mr. Borrett is seen receiving the Prunier Trophy from the Mayor of Lowestoft, Mr. Frank Jones at the Town Hall.

In 1963, the Yarmouth fishing vessel owner Bloomfields Ltd. ceased fishing and sold their six modern Lowestoft built drifter/trawlers to Small & Co. (Lowestoft) Ltd. Two of the six are featured here.

Left - The former *YH207 Ocean Cres*t in Lowestoft ownership and registered *LT468*. She was sold by Smalls in 1967 and became a research vessel. Later, *Ocean Crest* was sold to Anglo Spanish interests.

Below - Not long before being acquired by Small & Co., *YH167 Ocean Sunlight* is seen in the admired colour scheme adopted by her Yarmouth owners. In 1967, whilst in Dutch ownership she was lost with her crew.

Left - Two former Grimsby trawlers were added to the fleet in the late 1970s. One was built as *GY673 Tiberian*. Initially purchased by Lowestoft owner Colne Fishing, *Tiberian* passed into Smalls ownership in 1978. She became *LT 349 Suffolk Maid*, the second Small & Co. trawler to be so named. She was sold for possible use as a Caribbean trader in 1981, and was eventually sunk to form part of a reef.

Below - The steam drifter/trawler *LT152 Thrifty* was converted to diesel power in 1955. *Thrifty* passed to Fleetwood owners in 1960 and was allocated the fishing registration *FD201*. In 1967, she was renamed *Catherine Shaun*, and during 1971, was sold for scrapping.

When he was awarded the MBE in 1970, the well known and much respected Skipper Ernest "Jumbo" Fiske was one of few people to have been have decorated for services to the British fishing industry.
A top earning skipper in both drifting and trawling, he won the Prunier Trophy in 1964 in drifter/trawler *LT 671 Suffolk Warrior.* This vessel is featured on page 104.

Above - On the occasion of receiving the notification from Buckingham Palace of being awarded the MBE, Skipper Ernest Fiske is seen with his son, Skipper Richard Fiske, also a top skipper in drifters and trawlers.

Right - In 1970, Skipper E. Fiske retired and in the company of two members of his family, Skipper Eddy Brighty (on the left), and Skipper Richard Fiske (second left), he is seen with Company Chairman Major David Cartwright receiving his retirement gifts.

During 1978, the Royal Navy chartered two of the Small & Co stern trawlers, the *Suffolk Monarch* and *Suffolk Harvester*, for use on mine countermeasure trials work. The *Suffolk Monarch* became *HMS St. Davids*, and the *Suffolk Harvester* became *HMS Venturer*. Seen leaving Lowestoft under naval command is *HMS Venturer*. After five years, the former trawlers were returned to the Company and immediately converted for use on offshore support and survey work. They were sold in 1989.

The final years for the Company as a sea going concern saw its involvement with the offshore oil and gas industry. Three of the Company vessels involved in that work are featured here.

Top Left - Built for the Company, the supply ship *Suffolk Prince* is seen at Esbjerg in June 1982.

Top Right - The supply ship *Suffolk Kinsman* leaves Lowestoft. Formerly the *Cook Shore*, she was purchased in 1978.

Bottom Left - Just recognisable as a former stern trawler, the standby safety vessel *Suffolk Conquest* at Great Yarmouth. She is now the *Britannia Conquest*.

THE VESSELS

SOME OF THOSE OPERATED BY SMALL & CO. (LOWESTOFT) LTD., THEIR ASSOCIATED COMPANIES AND INDIVIDUAL OWNERS

The following log gives details of some of the sail, steam and diesel powered vessels that Small & Co. (Lowestoft) Ltd., or the Spashett family owned, or where known financial or business associations existed. Over the years, the ownership of a vast number of fishing and other vessels came to be associated with the Company, many of these through the Spashett family connection.

This log should **not** be considered as being conclusive. For some vessels suspected of having associations with the Company and/or the Spashetts, no proven or decisive ownership details remain, or are readily available. Vessels such as the *Celerity,* an iron built steamer dating from 1878, at one time in the part ownership of Frederick Spashett, and the sailing brigs operated by Captain Small in the mid 1800s have been omitted for this reason. A number of drifters and trawlers appear more than once, but with a different identity. In some cases, this reflects the identity before and after conversion from steam to diesel power. Almost all vessels with a name prefixed " Suffolk ", owned by Small & Co. (Lowestoft) Ltd. and their offshore subsidiary, Suffolk Marine are included. Two vessels, the large offshore supply ships *Pan Engineer* and *Pan Salvor*, reportedly purchased by Suffolk Marine in 1991, have been omitted. These vessels were purchased after the assets of the Company had been taken over by Britannia Marine. Both were renamed with the prefix "Britannia", and not "Suffolk", thereby following the naming policy of Britannia Marine, and not Suffolk Marine or Small & Co. (Lowestoft) Ltd. For a number of years, the movement of Company vessels in Lowestoft harbour was carried out by the small tug *Finch*, operated by Talisman Trawlers Ltd. Details of this tug may appear in a future publication. Please note that as with all titles in this series, the date given for the selling, transferring between subsidiaries, or disposal of a vessel, may only be approximate; for business reasons the actual date may be subject to commercial confidence.

Small & Co. trawlers *LT295 Suffolk Maid, LT422 Suffolk Craftsman* and *LT378 Suffolk Mariner* in the Trawl Dock at Lowestoft

Explanation of columns

Name The name carried by the vessel whilst part of Small & Co. (Lowestoft) Ltd., their associated companies and individual owner's fleets.

Fishing Registration The registration consisting of port letters and fishing numbers, as carried by the vessel when regularly fishing from Lowestoft. Explanation of the different port registrations can be found below in the "History" section.

Port Registration The port of registration for vessels other than drifters and trawlers e.g. Tugs, SSVs, barges, cargo and passenger vessels

Vessel Type As originally built

Official No. The official number of the vessel.

Call Sign The registered radio call sign.

Gross/Net Tonnage As recorded in official documentation. Given in imperial units.

Dimensions As recorded in official documentation. Given in imperial units and rounded to the nearest foot.

Construction The type of material used for the construction of the majority of the vessel.

Propulsion/Power Unit Main engine information. In this column, "E & G" refers to the Beccles machinery maker Elliott & Garrood.

Build Date The year the vessel was built.

Yard The yard at which the vessel was built.

Location The location of the yard. By special request, the yard numbers of Richards built vessels have been included.

History Highlights of the vessel's life, including any change in use. Particular emphasis is placed upon the time when she was a Lowestoft registered or based vessel. Included in this column are the following port distinguishing letters: -

A	Aberdeen	AR	Ayr
BCK	Buckie	BF	Banff
CTA	Capetown	D	Dublin
DH	Dartmouth	FD	Fleetwood
FR	Fraserburgh	GN	Granton
GY	Grimsby	H	Hull
HL	Hartlepool	IJM	Ymuiden
KY	Kirkcaldy	KW	Katwijk
LK	Lerwick	LO	London
LT	Lowestoft	LR	La Rochelle
M	Milford Haven	ML	Methil
N	Newry	PD	Peterhead
R	Ramsgate	SA	Swansea
SCH	Scheveningen	SY	Stornoway
WY	Whitby	WK	Wick
YH	Yarmouth (Norfolk)		

Abbreviations found in this column are as follows: -

BDSF	Boston Deep Sea Fisheries	EAI&CS	East Anglian Ice & Cold Storage Co. Ltd.
CWS	Cooperative Wholesale Society	HMD	His Majesty's Drifter
MMS	Motor Minesweeper	MVS	Maritime Voluntary Service
LV	Light Vessel	MOWT	Ministry of War Transport
PE	Putford Enterprises	RNMDSF	Royal National Mission to Deep Sea Fishermen
SSV	Standby Safety Vessel		

Name / Fishing Registration / Port Registration	Vessel Type / Call Sign / RSS/ON	Gross Tonnage / Net Tonnage	Dimensions (ft) / Construction	Propulsion Unit(s) / Make	Build Date / Build Yard / Build Location	History
Acceptable LT1291	Drifter/ Trawler GZPQ 130028	82 37	85 x 18 x 9 Steel	Steam Compound 32hp Crabtree	1911 Crabtree Gt. Yarmouth	Built as LT1125 for T. A. Utting 1914-18 War Service 1919 Sold to Thanet S. T. Co. Ltd., Ramsgate 1919 Allocated fishing registration R78 1924 Sold to County Fishing Co. Ltd., Lowestoft 1924 Allocated fishing registration LT1291 1953 Sold for scrapping
Amalia LT241	Trawler 149248	139 61	102 x 20 x 9 Steel	Steam Triple 270hp Ind. Maats	1917 Godreeders Leiderdorp	Built for Dutch owners 1930 In the ownership of Hobson & Co. Ltd 1930 Transferred to Vigilant Fishing Co. Ltd. 1939 Requisitioned by Admiralty for minesweeping 1939 Allocated pennant number FY1502 1945 Returned to owner in March 1946 Sold to Norway and renamed Eggoy 1949 Steam engine replaced by diesel
Annrobin LT203	Trawler MWBQ 187004	117 40	91 x 21 x 10 Steel	Diesel 1 x 6cyl 335hp Ruston	1955 Richards Lowestoft Yard No. 426	Built for East Anglian Ice & Cold Storage Co. Ltd. 1968 Transferred to Small & Co. (Lowestoft) Ltd. 1968 Sold to Sicily and was renamed Mary 1982 Ownership transferred to Guiseppi Quinci 1982 Registered at Mazara del Vallo
Ascona LT108	Drifter/ Trawler GWYY 149226	138 59	98 x 21 x 10 Steel	Steam Triple 51hp Crabtree	1929 Chambers Lowestoft	Built for N. G. & W. J. Utting 1939 Requisitioned by Admiralty for minesweeping 1939 Allocated pennant number FY949 1946 Sold to Vigilant Fishing Co. Ltd. 1953 Sold to Norrard Trawlers Ltd., Milford Haven 1957/8 Steam engine replaced by diesel. Work carried out by LBS Engineering, Lowestoft 1958 Left Lowestoft after conversion on 18th February 1970 Sold for scrapping at Blyth
B. R. Banks LT257	Trawler GNXX 183982	98 40	80 x 21 x 9 Steel	Diesel 1 x 4cyl 231hp Ruston	1951 Richards Lowestoft Yard No. 407	Built for East Anglian Ice & Cold Storage Co. Ltd 1966 Transferred to Small & Co. (Lowestoft) Ltd. in May 1966 Sold to Harry Herschel Glass, Capetown 1966 Left Lowestoft on 14th September 1966 Allocated fishing registration CTA158

Name Fishing Registration Port Registration	Vessel Type Call Sign RSS/ON	Gross Tonnage Net Tonnage	Dimensions (ft) Construction	Propulsion Unit(s) Make	Build Date Build Yard Build Location	History
Barkis Lowestoft	Tug 301358	63	64 x 19 x 6 Steel	Diesel 1 x 5cyl 325hp Ruston	1960 Yarwood Northwich	Built as Elmgarth for Rea Towing Co. Ltd. 1972 Sold to Pevensey Castle Ltd. 1972 Arrived at Lowestoft on 12th August 1972 Renamed Barkis in September 1976 Capsized and sank off Lowestoft on 16th August following a collision with MV Jupiter 1976 Wreck blown up
Ben & Lucy LT714	Drifter MQSS 129994	83 38	84 x 19 x 9 Steel	Steam Triple 25hp E & G	1910 Chambers Lowestoft	Built for B. Reynolds 1914-18 Requisitioned by Admiralty 1920 Transferred to V. Reynolds & Co. Ltd. 1925 Sold to H. Bond 1934 Transferred to Vigilant Fishing Co. Ltd. 1939 Requisitioned by Admiralty for minesweeping 1939 Allocated pennant number FY1511 1945 Returned to owner 1946 Sold to Norway 1950 Sold for scrap
Ben Iver LT788	Trawler GFFM 133640	197 77	116 x 22 x 12 Steel	Steam Triple 78hp Hall Russell	1913 Hall Russell Aberdeen	Built as A602 for R. Irvin & Sons Ltd., North Shields 1920 Purchased by Jack Breach Ltd. 1923 Sold and allocated fishing registration GN96 1925 Sold and allocated fishing registration A341 1939 In the ownership of J. Walker & others, Aberdeen 1947 In the ownership of G. Robb & Sons Ltd.
Boy Alan LT331	Drifter GYGB 136603	109 51	89 x 20 x 11 Wood	Steam Triple 25hp E & G	1914 Chambers Lowestoft	Built for Chas. Brittain 1919 Sold to J. V. Breach, A. Sago & B. Reynolds, 1921 Transferred to J. Breach, A. Sago & H. Reynolds 1921 Transferred to Boy Alan Ltd. 1938 Transferred to Kittiwake Ltd 1941 Sank after collision in Thames Estuary

Name Fishing Registration Port Registration	Vessel Type Call Sign RSS/ON	Gross Tonnage Net Tonnage	Dimensions (ft) Construction	Propulsion Unit(s) Make	Build Date Build Yard Build Location	History
Boy Nat LT1298	Drifter 132949	102 46	88 x 19 x 9 Steel	Steam Compound 35hp Crabtree	1912 Cochrane Selby	Built as LT1173 Hilda and Ernest for E. V. Snowling 1919 Sold To J. V. Breach, and R. G. Capps 1920 Sold to Thanet Steam Trawling Co. Ltd. 1920 Allocated fishing registration R116 1924 Sold to Frederick Spashett 1924 Allocated fishing registration LT1298 1924 Transferred to A. Catchpole and C. Allerton 1924 Transferred to Hobsons & Co. (Lowestoft) Ltd. 1924 Transferred to T. A. Utting 1924 Sank and refloated at Lowestoft on 30th June 1925 Renamed Available 1926 Sold to J. Innes, Buckie 1926 Allocated fishing registration BCK440 1939 In the ownership of W. Smith and others, Buckie
Boy Philip LT137	Drifter/ Trawler GWPX 149234	128 56	92 x 20 x 10 Steel	Steam Triple 39hp Crabtree	1930 Crabtree Gt. Yarmouth	Built for Pevensey Castle Ltd. 1939 Requisitioned by Admiralty for minesweeping and later, wreck dispersal work 1943 Returned to owner in August 1947 Sold to Anglo-Continental Fish Traders Ltd. 1947 Became GY44 Latania 1955 In the ownership of Norrand Trawlers Ltd. 1957 Steam engine replaced by diesel at Lowestoft
Boy Roy LT1167	Drifter 132940	94 42	86 x 19 x 10 Wood	Steam Triple 25hp E & G	1911 Chambers Lowestoft	Built for J. V. Breach 1914 Transferred to J. V. Breach & R. Soanes 1917 Transferred to J. V. Breach 1919 Transferred to Jack Breach Ltd. 1939 Requisitioned by Admiralty for use as a flare drifter 1940 Bombed and abandoned at Dunkirk on 28th May

| Name | Vessel Type | Gross Tonnage | Dimensions (ft) | Propulsion | Build Date | History |
| Fishing Registration | Call Sign | Net Tonnage | Construction | Unit(s) | Build Yard | |
Port Registration	RSS/ON			Make	Build Location	
Boy Scout	Drifter	79	82 x 18 x 9	Steam	1913	Built for E. Catchpole & Co. Ltd.
LT17	GYGB	39	Wood	Compound	Chambers	1914-18 War Service
	135739			20hp	Lowestoft	1929 Sold to T. A. Utting & Co. Ltd.
				E & G		1937 Transferred to T. Utting, George Spashett and T. Outlaw
						1939 Transferred to T. A. Utting
						1939 Requisitioned by Admiralty for use as a barrage balloon vessel
						1939 Allocated pennant number FY1865
						1944 Returned to owner in December
						1947 Sold to Greece
						1947 Left Lowestoft under tow on 27th June, became a total loss on passage to Greece
Boys Friend	Drifter/	120	94 x 20 x10	Steam	1915	Built as SCH135 Martina for W. den Dolk
LT151	Trawler	52	Steel	Triple	Godreeders	1922 Renamed Annie IJM8
	GYVG			275hp	Leiderdorp	1930 Acquired by Colls Durrant
	149233			Arnhemsche		1930 Became LT151 Boys Friend
						1936 Sold to Vigilant Fishing Co. Ltd., Lowestoft
						1955 Left Lowestoft for the shipbreakers on 26th September under tow
Byng	Drifter/	107	92 x 19 x 9	Steam	1919	Built as HMD Elephanta
LT632	Trawler	50	Steel	Triple	Fellows	1920 Purchased by Victory Fishing Co. Ltd
	GYPK			35hp	Gt. Yarmouth	1921 Transferred to Vigilant Fishing Co. Ltd.
	140000			Pertwee		1931 Sold to Keable Bros.
				& Back		1938 Sank at Lowestoft on 30th October
						1939 Transferred to G. W. Keable
						1939 Requisitioned by Admiralty
						1939 Assigned pennant number FY1870
						1939 In use as a boom defence and later, barrage balloon vessel
						1942 Transferred to Keable Bros.
						1944 Sold to Locarno Fishing Co. Ltd.
						1946 Returned to owner
						1955 Sold for scrapping at Antwerp
						1955 Left Lowestoft on 30th March with LT1290 Ramsey Bay in tow

Name Fishing Registration Port Registration	Vessel Type Call Sign RSS/ON	Gross Tonnage Net Tonnage	Dimensions (ft) Construction	Propulsion Unit(s) Make	Build Date Build Yard Build Location	History
Cape Colony LT22	Drifter 127604	82 38	85 x 19 x 9 Wood	Steam Compound 30hp Richards	1908 Richards Lowestoft Yard No. 140	Built for Colonial Fishing Co. Ltd. 1913 Sold to A. Duthie 1913 Allocated fishing registration FR525 1914-17 War Service 1917 Mined off Harwich on 8th January
Capetown LT76	Drifter 127608	82 38	85 x 19 x 9 Wood	Steam Compound 30hp Richards	1908 Richards Lowestoft Yard No. 142	Built for Colonial Fishing Co. Ltd. 1915-18 War Service 1918-20 Admiralty Service 1920 Sank as HMD Capetown off Cardigan Bay
Clansman Lowestoft	Cargo Ship 081960	302 141	150 x 22 x 11 Iron	Steam Compound 60hp Rowan & Sons	1880 Workman Clark Belfast	Built as Ethel (of Glasgow) 1889 In the ownership of D. MacBrayne, Glasgow 1917 Requisitioned by Admiralty for use as a collier 1919 Returned to owner in December 1921 Sold to Frederick Spashett 1923 Transferred to T. Small & Co. (Gt. Yarmouth) Ltd 1923 Transferred to Gt. Yarmouth Shipping Co. Ltd. 1924 Port of registry changed to Yarmouth 1926 Grounded on Haisbro Sand on 22nd October. On being refloated, she foundered due to water in the hold, the hatches having been smashed.
Colonial LT71	Drifter 127605	83 37	85 x 19 x 9 Wood	Steam Compound 30hp Crabtree	1908 Richards Lowestoft Yard No. 139	Built for Colonial Fishing Co. Ltd. 1920 Transferred to Britannia Fishing Co. Ltd. 1927 Sold to B. C. Burroughs 1928 Renamed Eastern Dawn 1935 Sold to G. Mitchell and H. Baxter 1938 Sold to P. W. Watson 1939 Requisitioned by Admiralty for de-gaussing use 1946 Returned to owner 1946 Abandoned at Whitstable 1951 Broken up on site
Constance Banks LT979	Trawler GXDH 309502	255 91	125 x 26 x 13 Steel	Diesel 1 x 6cyl 1100hp Ruston	1967 Appledore SB Appledore	Refer to Suffolk Sentinel for history

Name Fishing Registration Port Registration	Vessel Type Call Sign RSS/ON	Gross Tonnage Net Tonnage	Dimensions (ft) Construction	Propulsion Unit(s) Make	Build Date Build Yard Build Location	History
Craske Lowestoft	Barge 160684	82 62	81 x 15 x 8 Steel	Diesel 1 x 4cyl 180hp GM	1928 Alblasserdam	Built as Veracite 1949 Owned by Collisons Waterboat Co. Ltd., Hull 1949 Became Waterboat No. 9 1981 Purchased by Craske (Petroleum) Ltd. 1981 Arrived under tow at Lowestoft on 20th November 1982 Converted for use as a fuel barge
Devon County LT526	Drifter/ Yacht 129962	86 39	84 x 19 x 9 Wood	Steam Compound 31hp Crabtree	1910 Fellows Gt. Yarmouth	Built as LT526 Scadaun for Windham Thomas, Earl of Dunraven 1912 Sold to County Fishing Co. Ltd. 1912 Renamed Devon County 1914-1918 War Service 1939 Requisitioned by Admiralty for minesweeping 1941 Mined and sank in Thames Estuary on 1st July
Dewey LT59	Drifter 129601	83 36	84 x 19 x 8 Steel	Steam Compound 31hp Crabtree	1908 Crabtree Gt. Yarmouth	Built for Admiral Fishing Co. Ltd. 1914-18 War Service 1919 Sank on 12th August after a collision in the English Channel near the Royal Sovereign LV
Dick Whittington LT61	Drifter GZKM 135741	79 40	82 x 18 x 9 Wood	Steam Triple 20hp E & G	1913 Chambers Lowestoft	Built for Hayward & Co. Ltd. 1919 Transferred to J. C. Hayward 1929 Transferred to Kittiwake Ltd. 1948 Transferred to Black Cat Fishing Co. Ltd. 1950 Sold to Sea Scouts for £8 in April 1950 Very expensive for Scouts to run, broken up
Dick Whittington LT61	Drifter/ Trawler MTZF 186996	115 46	88 x 21 x 10 Steel	Diesel 1 x 5cyl 300hp Ruston	1955 Richards Lowestoft Yard No. 423	Built for Small & Co. (Lowestoft) Ltd. 1961 Prunier Trophy winner under Skipper Leo Borrett 1966 Whaleback fitted in December 1968 In use on SSV work 1968 Sold to Quincy & Asaro, Trapani 1968 Renamed Saturno II 1968 Left Lowestoft on 14th June with LT137 Norfolk Yeoman (Eros I)

| Name | Vessel Type | Gross Tonnage | Dimensions (ft) | Propulsion | Build Date | History |
| Fishing Registration | Call Sign | Net Tonnage | Construction | Unit(s) | Build Yard | |
Port Registration	RSS/ON			Make	Build Location	
Dorienta	Drifter	100	89 x 19 x 10	Steam	1914	Built as LT185 Happy Days for L. R. Tripp
LT185	GYVJ	49	Wood	Compound	Colby Bros	1914-18 War Service
	136575			20hp	Oulton Broad	1918 Sold to Strathon Drifters Ltd., Hartlepool
				E &G		1936 Sold to Vigilant Fishing Co. Ltd.
						1936 Transferred to J. C. Hayward and H. E. Smith
						1936 Renamed Dorienta
						1939 Requisitioned by Admiralty for minesweeping
						1939 Allocated pennant number FY705
						1945 Transferred to Vigilant Fishing Co. Ltd.
						1946 Returned to owner in May
						1948 Sold for breaking up
Drake	Drifter/	88	84 x 18 x 8	Steam	1907	Built for Admiral Fishing Co. Ltd.
LT1068	Trawler	29	Steel	Compound	Crabtree	1914-18 War Service as HMD Drake
				31hp	Gt. Yarmouth	1920 Sold to Thacker Bros.
	125860			Crabtree		1923 Renamed Retrieve
						1924 Sold to Maud Howard, Oulton Broad
						1928 Sold to R.G. Grant, Lerwick
						1928 Allocated fishing registration LK56
Eager	Drifter/	102	88 x 19 x 9	Steam	1912	Built for S. G. Allerton
LT1166	Trawler	46	Steel	Triple	Cochrane	1933 Part ownership transferred to Frederick Spashett
	MQVQ			35hp	Selby	1945 Sold to Bay Fisheries Ltd., Fleetwood
	132962			Cochrane		1947 Sold to H. B. Roberts, Lowestoft
						1951 Sold to Eager Fishing Co. Ltd., Lowestoft
						1953 Sold to W. H. Podd Ltd., Lowestoft
						1953 Transferred to Diesel Trawlers Ltd., Lowestoft
						1954 Steam engine replaced by 300hp AKD diesel
						1963 Sold to Gamashie Fishing & Marketing Co. Ltd., Accra, Ghana
East Anglia	Drifter	83	84 x 19 x 9	Steam	1909	Built for Dreadnought Fishing Co. Ltd.
LT328		35	Wood	Compound	Reynolds	1915-1919 War Service
	128634			32hp	Oulton Broad	1920 Sold to Portugal
				Crabtree		

Name Fishing Registration Port Registration	Vessel Type Call Sign RSS/ON	Gross Tonnage Net Tonnage	Dimensions (ft) Construction	Propulsion Unit(s) Make	Build Date Build Yard Build Location	History
Eileen Emma LT342	Drifter 136576	101 46	87 x 20 x 10 Wood	Steam Triple 25hp E & G	1914 Chambers Lowestoft	Built for J. Breach & E. Cooper 1914-18 War Service 1915 Rescued 116 people on 29th March off torpedoed SS Falaba in St. Georges Channel 1917 Transferred to J. V. Breach 1919 Transferred to Jack Breach Ltd. 1939 Requisitioned by Admiralty for auxiliary patrol use 1939 Allocated pennant number FY1992 1946 Returned to owner in April 1946 Sold to Norway and became Faaroy
Emerald LT437	Drifter 096492	47 20	72 x 18 x 7 Wood	Steam Compound 18hp Spence	1889 Mair Leith	1889 Allocated fishing registration SN61 1896 Sold and allocated fishing registration T861 1902 Sold to Lewis Strowger 1902 Allocated fishing registration LT437 1904 Sold to Frederick Spashett 1906 Sold to Fellows, Gt. Yarmouth 1906 Allocated fishing registration YH162 1911 Sold to C. T. Day 1911 Allocated fishing registration LT1133 1913 Lost on Scroby Sand on 28th October
Enterprise LT408	Drifter 122794	83 44	83 x 19 x 9 Wood	Steam Triple 25hp E & G	1906 Chambers Lowestoft	Built for J. Breach 1906 Transferred to J & J. V. Breach, F. Flowers, and W. Baxter 1914 Chartered by Admiralty, became Enterprise II 1916 Transferred to J & J. V Breach 1916 Mined and sank on 8th March
Ethel Mary LT337	Drifter/ Trawler MXSF 187017	133 56	92 x 22 x 9 Steel	Diesel 1 x 6cyl 360hp Ruston	1957 Richards Lowestoft Yard No. 436	Built for Small & Co. (Lowestoft) Ltd. 1957 Launched on 22nd June 1968 In use on SSV duties 1969 Sold to A. J. & A. Buchan, Fraserburgh 1970 Became FR186 Golden Promise 1970 Fishing for crayfish off Tristan da Cunha 1972 Returned to Fraserburgh 1974 Extensively modified and re-engined 1979 Sold to George Baird and George Taylor, Peterhead 1979 Became PD250 Magnificent 1998 Sold for scrapping at Inverness

Name	Vessel Type	Gross Tonnage	Dimensions (ft)	Propulsion	Build Date	History
Fishing Registration	Call Sign	Net Tonnage	Construction	Unit(s)	Build Yard	
Port Registration	RSS/ON			Make	Build Location	

Evening Primrose	Drifter	88	85 x 20 x 10	Steam	1911	Built for T. H. & A. J. Thirtle
LT1117	GJCR	38	Wood	Triple	Chambers	1914-18 War Service
	130024			25hp	Lowestoft	1918 Sold to A. B. Cullen
				E & G		1920 Sold to Colls Durrant
						1930 Sold to Vigilant Fishing Co. Ltd.
						1939 Requisitioned by Admiralty for minesweeping
						1939 Allocated pennant number FY1516
						1945 Returned to owner
						1947 Sold for breaking up at Oulton Broad
Expectant	Drifter	92	88 x 19 x 9	Steam	1913	Built for G. Hume
LT9	GZQL	45	Wood	Compound	Richards	1920 Sold to Lothian Trawling Co. Ltd.
	135742			30hp	Lowestoft	1927 Transferred to J. C. Hayward
				Richards	Yard No. 183	1929 Transferred to J. C. Hayward, A. Penman and George Spashett
						1939 Transferred to Kittiwake Ltd.
						1939 Sold for breaking up at Oulton Broad
Explorator	Drifter/	79	85 x 19 x 9	Steam	1909	Built as LT313 for Pye and Welton
LT515	Trawler	33	Wood	Triple	Reynolds	1914 Sold and allocated fishing registration ML12
				25hp	Lowestoft	1919 Sold to J. V. Breach
	128626			Crabtree		1919 Allocated fishing registration LT515
						1921 Transferred to Explorator Ltd.
						1925 Sold to W. J. Lockyer, Ramsgate
						1925 Allocated fishing registration R15
						1939 In the ownership of Albert Bachelor, Ramsgate
						1940 Broken up

The Ramsgate registered *Explorator*, rigged for trawling, leaving Lowestoft during the morning of 1st August 1928.

Name Fishing Registration Port Registration	Vessel Type Call Sign RSS/ON	Gross Tonnage Net Tonnage	Dimensions (ft) Construction	Propulsion Unit(s) Make	Build Date Build Yard Build Location	History
Feasible LT122	Drifter/ Trawler GYPQ 132963	103 46	86 x 19 x 9 Steel	Steam Triple 25hp E & G	1912 Torry SB Aberdeen	Built as LT1191 for W. Catchpole 1914 -19 War service as patrol drifter 1919 Sold to R. Kinnear, Doncaster 1919 Allocated fishing registration R157 1930 Sold to J. V. Breach Ltd. 1930 Allocated fishing registration LT122 1930 Transferred to J. V. Breach and J. S. Bush 1934 Transferred to J. V. Breach and A. J. Manthorpe 1935 Transferred to Jack Breach Ltd. 1938 Transferred to Explorator Ltd. 1939 Requisitioned by the Admiralty for minesweeping 1939 Assigned pennant number FY928 1945 Returned to owner 1945 Transferred to Pevensey Castle Ltd. 1946 Sold to Norway and became Meloy 1947 Steam engine replaced by a diesel 2000 In the ownership of River & Canal Pilotage Preservation Society
Fellowship LT246	Drifter/ Trawler GJPK 162951	127 52	94 x 20 x 9 Steel	Diesel 1 x 6cyl 335hp Ruston	1931 Goole SB Goole	Built as steam drifter/trawler Neves for Seven Ltd. 1937 Sold to Ritson J. Tripp, Kessingland 1939 Requisitioned by Admiralty for Harbour Duties 1945 Sold to County Fishing Co. Ltd., Lowestoft 1946 Returned to owner 1955 360hp steam engine replaced by 335hp diesel 1955 Renamed Fellowship 1961 Sold to J. J. Colby, S. Bond, D. Howes, R. Howes 1961 Transferred to Holkar Fishing Co. Ltd 1964 Transferred to Colby Fish Selling Co. Ltd. 1964 Funnel markings changed from "CHB" to "C" 1970 In use on SSV work 1975 Sold to Peter F. Horlock 1975 Left Lowestoft for Mistley 1975 Sold to Greece and later Arab interests 1987 Assumed no longer in existence

| Name | Vessel Type | Gross Tonnage | Dimensions (ft) | Propulsion | Build Date | History |
| Fishing Registration | Call Sign | Net Tonnage | Construction | Unit(s) | Build Yard | |
Port Registration	RSS/ON			Make	Build Location	

Fleurbaix
LT422
	Drifter/
	Trawler
	
	139985
		97
		41
			88 x 20 x 10
			Wood
				Steam
				Triple
				34hp
				Yeaman &
				Baggesen
					1919
					Colby Bros
					Oulton Broad
						Laid down as HMD Scud
						1919 Purchased by G. H. Bullimore
						    Named after the village where Major G. Spashett
						    was awarded the Military Cross
						1919 Sold to East Anglian Red Star Fishing Co. Ltd
						1926 Transferred to Jack Breach Ltd.
						1939 Sold for breaking up in Holland

Formidable LT100	Drifter 139977	87 40	86 x 20 x 9 Wood	Steam Compound 33hp Crabtree	1917 Chambers Lowestoft	Built for Frederick Spashett and W. Catchpole 1914-18 War Service 1918 Transferred to W. E. & E. Catchpole 1939 Requisitioned by Admiralty 1939 Became HMD Fidget 1946 Returned to owner 1946 Sold to Norway for use as a trader 1946 Left Lowestoft on 1st October 1946 Renamed Trix and steam engine replaced by diesel
Fort Albert LT357	Trawler 123359	192 74	112 x 22 x 12 Steel	Steam Triple 68hp A. Hall	1906 A. Hall Aberdeen	Built as A71 for Scottish owners 1914-18 War Service 1918 Sold to Frederick Spashett 1919 Transferred to County Fishing Co. Ltd. 1919 Allocated fishing registration LT357 1922 Sold to Aberdeen owners and became A932
Frederick Spashett LT138	Drifter/ Trawler MDZD 166725	97 40	81 x 21 x 9 Steel	Diesel 1 x 4cyl 231hp Ruston	1949 Richards Lowestoft Yard No. 388	Built for Small & Co. (Lowestoft) Ltd. 1953 Transferred to Vigilant Fishing Co. Ltd. 1956 Transferred to Trier Fishing Co. Ltd. 1965 Sold to Langusta Trawling Co. Ltd., Capetown 1967 Became Langusta II
Fume LT524	Drifter VRWF 139990	95 40	86 x 18 x 9 Steel	Steam Triple 43hp Yeaman & Baggesen	1919 Colby Bros Oulton Broad	Launched as HMD Fume 1919 Completed as a fishing vessel 1919 Purchased by Victory Fishing Co. Ltd. 1919 Became LT524 Fume 1921 Transferred to Vigilant Fishing Co. Ltd 1930 Sold to Raphael Fishing Co. Ltd., Port Louis, Mauritius 1930 Renamed Saint Pierre

| Name | Vessel Type | Gross Tonnage | Dimensions (ft) | Propulsion | Build Date | History |
| Fishing Registration | Call Sign | Net Tonnage | Construction | Unit(s) | Build Yard | |
Port Registration	RSS/ON			Make	Build Location	
Gervais Rentoul LT740	Drifter GKGV 132180	98 42	87 x 19 x 10 Wood	Steam Triple 42hp Beardmore	1917 Smith Buckie	Ordered for Admiralty 1919 Sold to Scottish owners, 1919 Became BCK237 Green Pasture 1920 Sold to J. V. Breach, E. Solomon and G. Spashett 1922 Transferred to J. V. Breach and Frederick Spashett 1923 Became LT740 Gervais Rentoul. Named after Conservative M. P. for North Suffolk 1925 Transferred to Explorator Ltd. 1939 Requisitioned by Admiralty for use as a flare drifter 1946 Returned to owner in May 1947 In the ownership of Don Fishing Co. Ltd, Aberdeen 1952 Broken up
Girl Gladys LT1174	Drifter GZPV 139978	110 58	88 x 20 x 10 Wood	Steam Compound 40hp Burrell	1917 Colby Bros Oulton Broad	Built for C. E. Day 1914-18 War Service 1919 Sold to East Anglian Red Star Fishing Co. Ltd. 1926 Transferred to Jack Breach Ltd. 1926 Transferred to Shoals Fishing Co. Ltd. 1939 Requisitioned by Admiralty for use as a flare drifter, also auxiliary and examination vessel use 1946 Returned to owner in February 1947 Broken up
Girls Friend LT171	Drifter 127619	55 32	74 x 19 x 8 Wood	Steam Compound 20hp E & G	1908 Chambers Lowestoft	Built for John Breach & Son Ltd. 1916 Stopped by a U boat 21 miles East of Hartlepool. Vessel destroyed by time bomb
Go Ahead LT534	Drifter GCCZ 139987	100 43	90 x 20 x 10 Wood	Steam Triple 43hp Burrell	1919 Colby Bros Oulton Broad	Built as HMD Volume 1919 Completed as LT534 Go Ahead 1919 Sold to East Anglian Red Star Fishing Co. Ltd. 1926 Transferred to Jack Breach Ltd. 1940 Lost on 18th Nov. after a collision off Sheerness
Golden Harvest LT1011	Drifter 136572	87 41	86 x 19 x 9 Wood	Steam Compound 25hp Richards	1914 Richards Lowestoft Yard No. 191	Built for Jas. Smith 1914-18 War Service 1920 Sold to J. R. Sutton 1939 Sold to Vigilant Fishing Co. Ltd. 1939 Requisitioned by Admiralty for minesweeping 1939 Allocated pennant number FY708 1946 Returned to owner in June 1947 Broken up

| Name | Vessel Type | Gross Tonnage | Dimensions (ft) | Propulsion | Build Date | History |
| Fishing Registration | Call Sign | Net Tonnage | Construction | Unit(s) | Build Yard | |
Port Registration	RSS/ON			Make	Build Location	
Good Hope LT564	Drifter 122751	67 35	81 x 18 x 8 Wood	Steam Compound 20hp Burrell	1905 Reynolds Lowestoft	Built for Chas. Harrington 1907 Sold to Britannia Fishing Co. Ltd. 1911 Sold to J .J. Colby 1911 Sold to A. Miller 1911 Allocated fishing registration YH756 1912 Sold to F. W. Stephen, Peterhead 1912 Allocated fishing registration BF516 1915-19 War Service 1920 Sold to Kennedy Robson & Co. Ltd., Stranraer 1921 Sold to J.H., A. J., & R. McMillan 1925 Broken up
Green Dolphin Lowestoft	Motor Minesweeper MRYL 166708	170 76	113 x 22 x 11 Wood	Diesel 1 x 7cyl 520hp British Polar	1941 Morris Gosport	Built for the Admiralty as MMS112 1947 Purchased by Vigilant Fishing Co. Ltd 1947 Converted for use as a passenger vessel 1947-48 In use as a pleasure craft at Lowestoft 1949 Sold to the Faroe Islands
George Spashett LT184	Drifter/ Trawler MKZT 183971	97 42	81 x 21 x 9 Steel	Diesel 1 x 4cyl 240hp Ruston	1950 Richards Lowestoft Yard No. 401	Built for Vigilant Fishing Co. Ltd. 1960 Transferred to Kittiwake Ltd. 1965 Sold to Langusta Trawling Co. Ltd., Capetown 1967 Renamed Langusta I
Happy Returns LT137	Drifter 104712	36	57 x 17 x 8 Wood	Sailing	1895 Porthleven	Built for J. Breach, F. Spashett and J. Allerton 1900 Transferred to J. Allerton 1920 Sold to R. C. Colby 1921 Sold to Belgium
Half Moon LT214	Drifter 132340	95 43 .	87 x 19 x 10 Wood	Steam Triple 25hp E & G	1911 Chambers Lowestoft	Built as YH729 for S. J. W. George 1914-18 War Service 1918 Sold to F. W. Hitchings and C. Gouldby 1919 Sold to R. Wylie 1919 Sold to East Anglian Red Star Fishing Co. Ltd 1927 Transferred to Jack Breach Ltd. 1936 Broken up

Name Fishing Registration Port Registration	Vessel Type Call Sign RSS/ON	Gross Tonnage Net Tonnage	Dimensions (ft) Construction	Propulsion Unit(s) Make	Build Date Build Yard Build Location	History
Harnser LT627	Drifter 139996	100 42	90 x 20 x 10 Wood	Steam Triple 28hp Carver	1919 Colby Bros Oulton Broad	Built as HMD Windhowl 1919 Completed as LT627 Harnser for East Anglian Red Star Fishing Co. Ltd 1926 Transferred to Jack Breach Ltd. 1939 Sold to Norway 1940 Steam engine replaced by diesel 1940 Renamed Anker I
Harold Cartwright LT231	Drifter/ Trawler GMDM 183974	97 57	86 x 21 x 9 Steel	Diesel 1 x 4cyl 231hp Ruston	1950 Richards Lowestoft Yard No. 402	Built for Pevensey Castle Ltd. 1966 Sold to H. Thon, Capetown 1966 Left Lowestoft on 17th September 1967 Renamed Pluto 1967 Sank in August, 15 miles south of Cape Agulhas
Henrietta Spashett LT82	Drifter/ Trawler GJBP 183958	97 40	81 x 19 x 9 Steel	Diesel 1 x 4cyl 231hp Ruston	1950 Richards Lowestoft Yard No. 389	Built for Seagull Fishing Co. Ltd. 1950 Transferred to the Small & Co. (Lowestoft) Ltd. 1952 Transferred to Vigilant Fishing Co. Ltd. 1966 Sold to A. A. van Wyk, Capetown 1966 Left Lowestoft on 14th September 1968 Fishing off Walvis Bay, South West Africa 1968 Grounded 2 miles N. of Palgrave Point on 14th July
Herring Searcher LT276	Drifter/ Trawler GZNR 135082	99 42	88 x 19 x 9 Steel	Steam Triple 33hp Crabtree	1914 Livingstone & Cooper Hessle	Built as YH51 for J. Salmon, Great Yarmouth 1928 Sold to Henry Eastick, Great Yarmouth 1939 Sold to Bisset Buchan Coull, Peterhead 1939 Allocated registration PD79 in May 1944 Sold to A. Johnstone, Gardenstown 1944 Allocated registration BF19 1947 Sold to Shoals Fishing Co. Ltd. Lowestoft 1947 Allocated registration LT276 1949 Prunier Trophy winner under Skipper S. Turrell 1954 Sold for scrapping 1954 Left Lowestoft on 9th June
John & Sarah LT289	Drifter 114998	60 36	80 x 18 x 8 Wood	Steam 20hp	1901 Chambers Lowestoft	Built for J. & J. V. Breach, L. Tripp and F. Spashett 1911 Total loss after a collision on 8th December with YH843 Ludham Castle. Broken up at Gorleston

Name Fishing Registration Port Registration	Vessel Type Call Sign RSS/ON	Gross Tonnage Net Tonnage	Dimensions (ft) Construction	Propulsion Unit(s) Make	Build Date Build Yard Build Location	History
John Alfred LT340	Drifter GTTG 135055	81 30	85 x 19 x 9 Wood	Steam Compound 24hp Carver	1913 Fellows Gt. Yarmouth	Built as YH350 Pleasants for H. Fenner Ltd. 1914-18 War Service 1927 Purchased by Jack Breach Ltd. 1927 Allocated fishing registration LT340 1939 Requisitioned by Admiralty for minesweeping 1939 Allocated pennant number FY1518 1945 Returned to owner 1946 In the ownership of Shoals Fishing Co. Ltd. 1947 Broken up in Belgium
John Alfred LT470	Drifter 129951	81 34	84 x 19 x 9 Wood	Steam Compound 20hp Burrell	1909 Chambers Lowestoft	Built for J. & J. V. Breach 1914-18 War Service 1917 Transferred to J. V. Breach 1919 Transferred to Jack Breach Ltd 1927 Run down and sunk off Shields on 19th May
Kent County LT1129	Drifter 130040	85 39	84 x 18 x 9 Steel	Steam Compound 32hp Crabtree	1911 Cochrane Selby	Built for County Fishing Co. Ltd. 1914 Requisitioned by Admiralty for Q ship work 1916 Mined and sunk on 8th December off Cross Sand LV. Eleven crew lost
Kent County LT106	Drifter 149222	128 56	92 x 20 x 10 Steel	Steam Triple 39hp Crabtree	1929 Crabtree Gt. Yarmouth	Built for County Fishing Co. Ltd. 1932 Sold to Dublin Port & Docks Board for pilot cutter use 1964 Sold for scrapping
Kiddaw LT361	Drifter GKRW 128632	86	85 x 19 x 9 Steel	Steam Compound 31hp Crabtree	1909 Fellows Gt. Yarmouth	Built as Ruler of the Sea for Britannia Fishing Co. Ltd. 1927 Transferred to Seagull Fishing Co. Ltd. 1937 In the ownership of Jack Breach Ltd. 1939 Requisitioned by Admiralty for use as a barrage balloon vessel 1939 Allocated pennant number FY1877 1945 Returned to owner in July 1947 In the ownership of Britannia Fishing Co. Ltd. 1949 Last year of fishing 1951 Sold for scrapping

Name	Vessel Type	Gross Tonnage	Dimensions (ft)	Propulsion	Build Date	History
Fishing Registration	Call Sign	Net Tonnage	Construction	Unit(s)	Build Yard	
Port Registration	RSS/ON			Make	Build Location	
Lanner	Drifter	103	90 x 19 x 9	Steam	1912	Built for J. Utting
LT1176	GZYW	43	Steel	Triple	Torry SB	1914-18 War Service
	132951			42hp	Aberdeen	1919 Sold to Ploughboy Co. Ltd.
				Ledgerwood		1937 Transferred to Kittiwake Ltd.
						1939 Requisitioned by Admiralty for minesweeping
						service in the Mediterranean
						1946 Returned to owner
						1947 Sold for scrapping
Lavinia L	Drifter	72	81 x 19 x 9	Steam	1917	Built for J. B. Laverick
LT1299	GZYK	31	Wood	Compound	Chambers	1923 Sold to W. Strowger
	137075			24hp	Lowestoft	1924 Sold to Resolute Fishing Co. Ltd.
				Carver		1926 Transferred to E. Catchpole (Grassholme Synd.)
						1938 Transferred to Vigilant Fishing Co. Ltd.
						1939 Requisitioned by Admiralty
						1941 Bombed and sunk at Sheerness
Leonard Cockrell	Trawler	130	91 x 22 x 9	Diesel	1958	Built for East Anglian Ice & Cold Storage Co. Ltd.
LT34		51	Steel	1 x 6cyl	Richards	1971 Sold to Cyprus
	187036			360hp	Lowestoft	1971 Left Lowestoft on 13th March
				Ruston	Yard No. 443	1971 Renamed Aghios Constaninos Alamanos
Linsdell	Drifter	88	84 x 19 x 9	Steam	1914	Built for Frederick Spashett and J. Utting
LT322		38	Wood	Compound	Chambers	1914 Requisitioned by Admiralty
	124439			32hp	Lowestoft	1914 Mined on 3rd September off the Outer
				Crabtree		Dowsing L V. Five crew lost
Loch Broom	Trawler	197	112 x 22 x 12	Steam	1907	Built as A141 for Scottish owners
LT327		75	Steel	Triple	A. Hall	1919 Purchased by G. C. Hall
	123784			60hp	Aberdeen	1919 Transferred to Resolute Fishing Co. Ltd.
				A. Hall		1923 Sold to Spain
						1923 Renamed Santa Clara
Loch Eriboll	Trawler	211	116 x 27 x 12	Steam	1915	1919 Purchased by Resolute Fishing Co. Ltd. as A546
LT707		78	Steel	Triple	A. Hall	1921 Sold to Scottish owners
	137183			69hp	Aberdeen	1921 Allocated fishing registration A683
				A. Hall		

Name Fishing Registration Port Registration	Vessel Type Call Sign RSS/ON	Gross Tonnage Net Tonnage	Dimensions (ft) Construction	Propulsion Unit(s) Make	Build Date Build Yard Build Location	History
London County LT329	Drifter 128628	82 36	84 x 19 x 9 Wood	Steam Compound 25hp Davis	1909 Chambers Lowestoft	Built for County Fishing Co. Ltd. 1914-18 War Service 1919 Total loss on 28th October after running ashore at Beadnell whilst on passage from Russia to Aberdeen
Lurline LT658	Trawler 089043	65	73 x 19 x 9 Wood	Sailing	1884 Hoad Rye	Built as YH911 for W. H. Willis, Gorleston 1891 Sold to J. Williams 1895 Sold to Frederick Spashett 1895 Sold to W. Robbins and A. Brereton 1902 Sold to Frederick Spashett 1902 Sold to W. Wright 1903 Lost 2 miles SE of Corton LV on 23rd September after being in collision with SS Perth (of Dundee)
Madame Prunier LT343	Drifter/ Trawler MAVW 181489	119 51	86 x 20 x 11 Wood	Diesel 1 x 4cyl 265hp Crossley	1948 Brooke Marine Oulton Broad	Launched as Madame Prunier Completed as PD388 Equity I for Scottish CWS 1952 Sold to the Clan Steam Fishing Co. (Grimsby) Ltd. 1952 Registered as LT343 1953 Renamed Madame Prunier 1953 Sold to Pevensey Castle Ltd. 1959 Sold to G. Doyle, Howth 1961 Renamed Croidte Au Duin 1966 Registered as N198 1968 Registered as D190 1990 Scrapped at Kilkeel
Majesty LT66	Drifter 127606	84 37	84 x 18 x 8 Steel	Steam Compound 31hp Crabtree	1908 Crabtree Gt. Yarmouth	Built for Britannia Fishing Co. Ltd. 1914-18 War Service 1926 Sold to J. Mowat, Seatown 1926 Allocated fishing registration BF174 1939 Owned by J. Mowat and W. Mowat, Cullen 1939 Requisitioned by Admiralty for minesweeping 1939 Allocated pennant number FY1597 1946 Returned to owner in September

Name Fishing Registration Port Registration	Vessel Type Call Sign RSS/ON	Gross Tonnage Net Tonnage	Dimensions (ft) Construction	Propulsion Unit(s) Make	Build Date Build Yard Build Location	History
Margaret Hide LT746	Drifter/ Trawler GRVD 140021	160 68	103 x 21 x 11 Steel	Steam Triple 56hp Beardmore	1920 Torry SB Aberdeen	Built for J. V. Breach, named after his mother 1921 Transferred to Pevensey Castle Ltd., Lowestoft 1939 Requisitioned by Admiralty 1939 Allocated Pennant Number FY981 1945 Returned to owner in April 1954 Last year of fishing 1955 Sold for scrapping 1955 Left Lowestoft on 26th Sept. for Belgium breakers with LT151 Boys Friend in tow
Margaret Christina LT331	Trawler GHDY 302388	137 48	92 x 22 x 9 Steel	Diesel 1 x 6cyl 360hp Ruston	1960 Richards Lowestoft Yard No. 459	Built for East Anglian Ice & Cold Storage Co. Ltd. 1969 Transferred to Small & Co. (Lowestoft) Ltd. 1970 Sold to Southern Marine Ltd. Malahide, ROI 1970 Fishing registration cancelled, registered in Dublin 1971 Sold to Putford Enterprises Ltd. 1971 Allocated fishing registration LT331 1975 Converted for use as a SSV 1983 Sank near Leman Bank 1983 Wreck raised due to being near undersea gas pipe 1983 Taken to Rotterdam for scrapping by Taklift 4 1983 Arrived on 22nd October
Marinus LT240	Drifter GZNN 145826	92 41	86 x 19 x 9 Steel	Steam Triple 27hp Crabtree	1925 Cochrane Selby	Built for Seagull Fishing Co. Ltd. 1929 Sold to E. T. Capps 1929 Renamed Justified 1939 Requisitioned by Admiralty 1941 Transferred to MOWT in October 1942 Mined and Sank off Malta on 16th June
Marinus LT1150	Drifter 130050	84 37	83 x 18 x 9 Steel	Steam Compound 32hp Crabtree	1911 Crabtree Gt. Yarmouth	Refer to Touchwood for history

Name Fishing Registration Port Registration	Vessel Type Call Sign RSS/ON	Gross Tonnage Net Tonnage	Dimensions (ft) Construction Make	Propulsion Unit(s)	Build Date Build Yard Build Location	History
Mary Bruce LT368	Trawler MFRL 129283	207 82	112 x 22 x 12 Steel	Steam Triple 45hp Amos & Smith	1910 Cook, Welton & Gemmell Beverley	Built as H131 Pericles for Hellyers S. T. Co. Ltd. 1919 Sold to Hull Northern Fishing Co. Ltd. 1928 Ocean Steam Fishing Co. Ltd., Milford Haven 1936 Sold to A. R. Buthlay & others, Aberdeen 1936 Became A393 Mary Bruce 1943 Sold to Fort Rona Fishing Co. Ltd. 1947 Allocated fishing registration M147 1947 In the ownership of United Trawlers Ltd. 1948 Purchased by Shoals Fishing Co. Ltd. 1948 Allocated fishing registration LT368 1953 Sold for scrapping on the Tyne
Mary Heeley LT308	Trawler GZMJ 165441	162 60	101 x 21 x 10 Steel	Steam Triple 41hp Crabtree	1937 Goole SB Goole	Built as LO197 Edward P. Wills for the RNMDSF 1939-45 War Service 1949 Sold to Vigilant Fishing Co. Ltd. in August 1949 Allocated fishing registration LT308 1950 Renamed Mary Heeley 1950 Wrecked during the night of 29/30th April in fog near Douglas Bay, Isle of Man. Total loss.
Mascot LT1038	Drifter 125859	62 25	74 x 18 x 8 Wood	Steam Compound 20hp E & G	1907 Chambers Lowestoft	Built for A. Gouldby, Graves & Co. Ltd. 1918 Sold to J.V. Breach and R. C. Capps 1919 Transferred to Jack Breach Ltd. 1927 Total loss on 5th August after running ashore in fog at Hartlepool
Meg LT316	Drifter 120363	82 25	82 x 19 x 9 Wood	Steam Compound 24hp Carver	1906 Fellows Gt. Yarmouth	Built as YH397 for H. J. Sayers 1909 Sold to C. & A. Harvey 1909 Allocated fishing registration LT316 1910 Sold to A. W. H., C. H. & T. J. Kemp 1913 Transferred to A. W. H. & T. J. Kemp 1914-18 War Service 1919 Transferred to A. W. H. Kemp 1919 Sold to Victory Fishing Co. Ltd. 1921 Transferred to Vigilant Fishing Co. Ltd. 1936 Total loss on 5th June after breaking loose whilst undertow and running ashore north of Scarborough

Name Fishing Registration Port Registration	Vessel Type Call Sign RSS/ON	Gross Tonnage Net Tonnage	Dimensions (ft) Construction	Propulsion Unit(s) Make	Build Date Build Yard Build Location	History
Merry Spinner LT1150 130050	Drifter	84 37	83 x 18 x 9 Steel	Steam Compound 32hp Crabtree	1911 Crabtree Gt. Yarmouth	Refer to Touchwood for history
Nell Morgan LT448 098947	Trawler	68	77 x 20 x 10 Wood	Sailing	1885 Reynolds Lowestoft	Built as YH1048 for W. Morgan, Gorleston 1891 Sold to J. S. Sterry 1891 Allocated fishing registration LT448 1899 Sold to E. Beck 1899 Sold to Frederick Spashett 1901 Sold to W. Robbens 1903 Sold to Sweden 1906 Sold to Norway 1926 Wrecked
Nelson LT516 124399	Drifter	70 34	80 x 17 x 8 Wood	Steam Compound 28hp Crabtree	1906 Fellows Gt. Yarmouth	Built for Admiral Fishing Co. Ltd 1915-1919 War Service 1920 Sold to G. A. Foster, A. Mitchell and E. Yallop 1925 Sold to Spain
Netsukis LT271	Drifter GJQG 135772	85 39	83 x 19 x 9 Wood	Steam Compound 30hp Crabtree	1913 Chambers Lowestoft	Built for White Star Fishing Co. Ltd. 1914-18 War Service 1931 Transferred to Vigilant Fishing Co. Ltd. 1939 Requisitioned by Admiralty for auxiliary patrol and later, torpedo recovery use 1939 Allocated pennant number FY1971 1946 Returned to owner in April 1947 Broken up
Neves LT246	Drifter/ Trawler GJPK 162951	121 61	94 x 20 x 9 Steel	Steam Triple 360hp E & G	1931 Goole SB Goole	Refer to Fellowship for history
Nil Desperandum LT175 117485	Drifter	80 38	89 x 19 x 8 Wood	Steam Triple 25hp E & G	1903 Chambers Lowestoft	Built for J. V. & J. Breach and L. R.Tripp 1908 Transferred to J. V. Breach and J. Breach 1917 Transferred to J. Breach 1919 Transferred to Jack Breach Ltd. 1936 Broken up at Oulton Broad

Name	Vessel Type	Gross Tonnage	Dimensions (ft)	Propulsion	Build Date	History
Fishing Registration	Call Sign	Net Tonnage	Construction	Unit(s)	Build Yard	
Port Registration	RSS/ON			Make	Build Location	

Norfolk County
LT103

	Drifter/	83	84 x 18 x 8	Steam	1908	Built for County Fishing Co. Ltd.
	Trawler	35	Steel	Compound	Cochrane	1914-18 War Service
				31hp	Selby	1939 Requisitioned by Admiralty for target service
	127618			Crabtree		1945 Returned to owner

Norfolk County — continued:
1946 Sold to Norway and renamed Stodraat, later
the steam engine was replaced by a diesel
2001 Purchased and returned to the UK

Norfolk Yeoman
LT137

	Drifter/	114	88 x 21 x 10	Diesel	1955	Built for Small & Co. Ltd. (Lowestoft) Ltd.
	Trawler	46	Steel	1 x 5cyl	Richards	1963 Prunier Trophy winner under Skipper R. Sims
	MTZC			300hp	Lowestoft	1966 Whaleback fitted in December
	186999			Ruston	Yard No. 424	1967 One of only two Company drifters herring fishing

1967 Under Skipper Meen landed herring worth £13,956
1968 In use on SSV work
1968 Sold to Leonardo and Asaro, Trapani
1968 Became Eros I
1968 left Lowestoft on 14th June with Dick Whittington
1973 Renamed Eros Primo

Ocean Crest
LT468

	Drifter/	131	91 x 21 x 10	Diesel	1956	Built as YH207 for Bloomfields Ltd., Great Yarmouth
	Trawler	63	Steel	1 x 6cyl	Richards	1963 Sold to Small & Co. (Lowestoft) Ltd.
	GVWL			360hp	Lowestoft	1963 Fishing registration changed to LT468
	187910			Ruston	Yard No. 433	1967 Sold to University College of Swansea

1967 Left Lowestoft for Sheerness on 31st August
1967 Fishing registration cancelled
1967 Reclassified as a research/survey vessel
1984 Sold to Emmaledes Ltd., Penzance
1984 Allocated fishing registration SA110

Name	Vessel Type	Gross Tonnage	Dimensions (ft)	Propulsion	Build Date	History
Fishing Registration	Call Sign	Net Tonnage	Construction	Unit(s)	Build Yard	
Port Registration	RSS/ON			Make	Build Location	
Ocean Dawn	Drifter/	131	91 x 21 x 10	Diesel	1956	Built as YH77 for Bloomfields Ltd., Great Yarmouth
LT466	Trawler	63	Steel	1 x 6cyl	Richards	1963 Sold to East Anglian Ice and Cold Storage Co. Ltd
	MWVG			360hp	Lowestoft	1963 Registered LT466 on 21st February
	186405			Ruston	Yard No. 431	1968 Transferred to Small & Co. (Lowestoft) Ltd.
						1969 Sold to James Muir, Anstruther
						1969 Sailed for Cellardyke on the 2nd September
						1969 Allocated registration KY371
						1979 Sank in Aberdeen on 10th September
						1979 Raised on 19th September
						1984 Sold to Colne Shipping Co. Ltd. in March
						1984 Fishing registration cancelled
						1984 Converted for use as a SSV
						1984 Renamed Rewga (of Lowestoft)
						1987 Sold to Mats Lilja, Sweden
						1987 Left Lowestoft for Sweden on 24th February
						1988 Renamed Ocean Dawn
						1991 Advertised for sale at £65,000 in the spring
						1991 Advertised for sale at £45,000 in the autumn
						1998 Sold to Mr. J. Price, Shoreham
						2000 In the ownership of Mr. S. Robertson
Ocean Starlight	Drifter/	114	88 x 21 x 11	Diesel	1952	Built as YH61 for Bloomfields Ltd., Great Yarmouth
LT465	Trawler	46	Steel	1 x 6cyl	Richards	1962 Prunier Trophy winner under Skipper S. Hewitt
	GQBK			360hp	Lowestoft	1963 Sold to Small & Co. (Lowestoft) Ltd.
	185677			Ruston	Yard No. 410	1963 Registration changed to LT465
						1967 Sold to J. Hoek of Ymuiden
						1967 Left Lowestoft on 29th September
						1967 Became KW38 Neptunus
						1970 Sold to J. Van Lear of Ymuiden
						1970 Renamed Dolfijn
						1970 Fishing registration closed
						1970 In use as a SSV
						1972 Sold to P.F. G.A. & F.E.Catchpole and J.Hashim
						1972 Arrived at Lowestoft on 17th February
						1972 Became LT465 Stoic
						1975 Transferred to the Warbler Fishing Co. Ltd.
						1976 Fully converted for use as a SSV
						1981 Renamed Dawn Spray
						1987 Sold to Norrand Trawlers Ltd., Milford Haven
						1992 Under detention and for sale at Milford Haven
						1995 Sold for scrapping

Name	Vessel Type	Gross Tonnage	Dimensions (ft)	Propulsion	Build Date	History
Fishing Registration	Call Sign	Net Tonnage	Construction	Unit(s)	Build Yard	
Port Registration	RSS/ON			Make	Build Location	
Remembrance	Drifter	81	84 x 19 x 9	Steam	1910	Built for J. & J. V. Breach
LT544		35	Wood	Triple	Chambers	1914-18 War Service
	129971			25hp	Lowestoft	1917 Transferred to J. V. Breach
				E & G		1919 Transferred to Jack Breach Ltd.
						1919 Sold to M. Mcleod
						1919 Allocated fishing registration SY21
						1921 Declared a total loss
Resolute	Drifter	48	67 x 17 x 9	Steam	1886	Built as LH3 for W. Wilcox, Manchester
LT960		18	Wood	Compound	McKenzie	1914 Sold to J. E. Harper and J. R. McDonald, Wick
	091085			10hp	Leith	1914 Allocated fishing registration WK45
				Cran		1917 Sold to R. B. Bradbeer, Lowestoft
						1917 Allocated fishing registration LT960
						1918 Sold to A. Cullen
						1919 Sold to G. Hall and H. Baxter
						1919 Sold to Resolute Fishing Co. Ltd.
						1919 Sold to C. H. Margason, Grimsby
						1921 Sold and converted to a lighter
Retriever	Drifter/	89	84 x 18 x 8	Steam	1909	Built as LT1096 for J & T Belton
LT120	Trawler	38	Steel	Compound	Crabtree	1920 Sold to J. H. Wood
	GPGS			31hp	Gt. Yarmouth	1920 Allocated fishing registration KY34
	125890			Crabtree		1930 Sold to Explorator Ltd
						1930 Became LT120 Score Head
						1930 Transferred to Pevensey Castle Ltd
						1946 Sold to H. Roberts and R. Sprake
						1949 Transferred to G. Dicker and R. Sprake
						1949 Last year of fishing
						1951 Sold for scrapping
Reunited	Drifter	83	88 x 18 x 9	Steam	1912	Built as FR511 for J. Hay and others
LT68		34	Wood	Triple	Geddes	1929 Purchased by Kittiwake Ltd as R51 George Hay
	125339			35hp	Portgordon	1929 Became LT68 Reunited
				Lewis		1938 Foundered in heavy weather on 28th November

Name	Vessel Type	Gross Tonnage	Dimensions (ft)	Propulsion	Build Date	History
Fishing Registration	Call Sign	Net Tonnage	Construction	Unit(s)	Build Yard	
Port Registration	RSS/ON			Make	Build Location	

Reverberation	Drifter	97	87 x 20 x 10	Steam	1919	Built for Admiralty and completed as a fishing vessel
LT369		41	Wood	Triple	Colby Bros	1919 Sold to G. H. Bullimore
	139981			36hp	Oulton Broad	1919 Transferred to East Anglian Red Star
				N. British		Fishing Co. Ltd.
						1926 Transferred to Jack Breach Ltd.
						1939 Requisitioned by Admiralty for auxiliary
						patrol duties
						1939 Allocated pennant number FY1990
						1945 Returned to owner in February
						1946 In the ownership of Shoals Fishing Co. Ltd.
						1947 Broken up
Reward	Drifter		83 x 19 x 9	Steam	1906	Built for R and J. G. Utting
LT 463		42	Wood	Compound	Richards	1914-18 War Service
	124396			42hp	Lowestoft	1917 Sold to J. V. Breach
				Richards	Yard No. 123	1919 Transferred to Jack Breach Ltd.
						1929 Sank in Yarmouth Roads on 5th December after
						grounding, and being refloated in Corton Roads
Rising Sun	Trawler	50	66 x 18 x 9	Sailing	1880	Built for J. S. Macey
LT194			Wood		Hoad	1899 Sold to Frederick Spashett & E. Beck
	082377				Rye	1900 Sold to Norway
						1902 Sold to Iceland
						1902 Became Pollux (of Hafnarfjord)
						1911 Became Pollux (of Bardastrandarsysla)
Rissa	Drifter	99	88 x 20 x 10	Steam	1912	Built as YH692 Thomas Beeching for Gt. Yarmouth
LT52		34	Wood	Triple	Beeching Bros	Steam Drifters Ltd. and W. Miles
	132377			28hp	Gt. Yarmouth	1920 Transferred to Gt. Yarmouth Steam Drifters Ltd.
				Carver		1924 Sold to Seagull Fishing Co. Ltd
						1924 Became LT52 Rissa
						1925 Sold to T. Reid, Portgordon
						1925 Allocated fishing registration BCK103
						1933 Foundered on 3rd December off St. Combs whilst
						returning home from East Anglia

Name	Vessel Type	Gross Tonnage	Dimensions (ft)	Propulsion	Build Date	History
Fishing Registration	Call Sign	Net Tonnage	Construction	Unit(s)	Build Yard	
Port Registration	RSS/ON			Make	Build Location	

Rodney	Drifter	81	84 x 19 x 9	Steam	1907	Built for Admiral Fishing Co. Ltd.
LT1042		33	Wood	Compound	Reynolds	1913 Sold to H. Baxter
	124440			24hp	Oulton Broad	1914-18 War Service
				Carver		1914 Sold to J. Dougall, Eyemouth
						1923 Foundered off Craster on 29th September

Rooke	Drifter	83	84 x 18 x 8	Steam	1908	Built for Admiral Fishing Co. Ltd.
LT53		36	Steel	Compound	Crabtree	1914-16 War Service
	127594			31hp	Gt. Yarmouth	1916 Total loss on 3rd August after a collision off Deal
				Crabtree		

Roy Stevens	Trawler	202	107 x 23 x 11	Diesel	1961	Built for Explorator Ltd.
LT271	GHDZ	66	Steel	1 x 6cyl	Richards	1964 Transferred to Small & Co. (Lowestoft) Ltd
	302393			550hp	Lowestoft	1974 Sold to BDSF
				Ruston	Yard No. 458	1974 Renamed Boston Aztec
						1980 Sold and renamed Fahnous

Sarah Hide	Drifter/	162	103 x 21 x 11	Steam	1921	Built as LT1215 Arthur Gouldby for Arthur Gouldby
LT1157	Trawler	68	Steel	Triple	Torry SB	1922 Transferred to Arthur Gouldby and others
	GCCQ			56hp	Aberdeen	1937 Sold to Kittiwake Ltd
	140025			Beardmore		1937 Became LT1157 Sarah Hide
						1939 Requisitioned by Admiralty for minesweeping and later auxiliary patrol use
						1939 Allocated pennant number FY968
						1946 Returned to owner in January
						1955 Sold for scrapping
						1955 Left Lowestoft on 31st January for Belgium breakers

Sarah Marian	Drifter	89	86 x 20 x 10	Steam	1911	Built for J. V. Breach and J. Breach
LT1119		38	Wood	Compound	Chambers	1914-18 War Service
	130015			20hp	Lowestoft	1917 Transferred to J. V. Breach
				E & G		1919 Transferred to Jack Breach Ltd.
						1920 Run down by Girl Gladys on 15th December and sank whilst anchored in Lowestoft Roads

Name Fishing Registration Port Registration	Vessel Type Call Sign RSS/ON	Gross Tonnage Net Tonnage	Dimensions (ft) Construction	Propulsion Unit(s) Make	Build Date Build Yard Build Location	History
Scadaun LT1183 132959	Drifter	107 46	93 x 21 x 10 Wood	Steam Triple 35hp Crabtree	1912 Chambers Lowestoft	Built for Lord Dunraven 1917 In the ownership of Capt. Lucas 1921 Transferred to County Fishing C. Ltd. 1933 Total loss after hitting submerged rock on 5th August near Castebay Harbour. Crew saved
Scarborough LT240 110796	Drifter	54 30	76 x 17 x 8 Wood	Steam Compound 15hp E & G	1900 Chambers & Colby Lowestoft	Built as H502 for British Coast Fishing Co. Ltd. 1916 Sold to Scottish owners 1916 Allocated fishing registration FR276 1918 Sold to Frederick Spashett 1918 Allocated fishing registration LT240 1918 Foundered 16 miles from Haisbro L.V.
Scania LT621 140023	Drifter	94 21	87 x 20 x 10 Wood	Steam Triple 46hp Cooper & Greig	1919 Stevenson & Asher Banff	Refer to Taal Hina for history
Score Head LT120	Drifter/ Trawler GPGS 125890	89 38	84 x 18 x 8 Steel	Steam Compound 31hp Crabtree	1907 Crabtree Gt. Yarmouth	Refer to Retriever for history
Searcher LT290 128610	Drifter	58 34	75 x 18 x 8 Wood	Steam Compound 20hp E & G	1908 Chambers Lowestoft	Built for J. Breach and J. V. Breach 1914-18 War Service 1915 Transferred to J. V. Breach 1919 Transferred to Jack Breach Ltd. 1937 Sold for breaking up
Shipmates LT1134	Drifter GYRY 130036	82 37	84 x 18 x 9 Steel	Steam Compound 32hp Crabtree	1911 Crabtree Gt. Yarmouth	Built for Frederick Spashett 1912 Sold to G. A. Snowling 1915 Requisitioned by Admiralty 1916 Sold to Frederick Spashett 1918 Sold to H. Utting 1919 Returned to owner 1939 Requisitioned by Admiralty 1939 In use as a flare drifter 1940 Sunk by enemy aircraft at Dover on 14th November

Name Fishing Registration Port Registration	Vessel Type Call Sign RSS/ON	Gross Tonnage Net Tonnage	Dimensions (ft) Construction	Propulsion Unit(s) Make	Build Date Build Yard Build Location	History
Silver Spray LT294	Trawler	75	73 x 20 x 10 Wood	Sailing	1875 Wray Burton Stather	1889 Owned by Mrs Butler 1900 Sold to Frederick Spashett 1901 Sold to William Bird, Guernsey
Skimmer of the Sea LT768	Trawler 065149	46	64 x 17 x 9 Wood	Sailing	1871 Pardew Plymouth	1874 Allocated fishing registration DH814 1898 Sold to Frederick Spashett and R. Rivett 1898 Allocated fishing registration LT768 1899 Lost on Holm Sand on 8th February
Sternus LT238	Drifter/ Trawler GYPP 145827	93 41	86 x 19 x 9 Steel	Steam Triple 27hp Crabtree	1925 Cochrane Selby	Refer to LT238 Swiftwing for history
Strathderry LT532	Trawler GKVT 129364	192 74	113 x 22 x 12 Steel	Steam Triple 67hp Hall Russell	1911 Hall Russell Aberdeen	Built as A401 for Scottish owners 1914-18 War Service 1919 Returned to owners 1919 Sold to Frederick Spashett 1919 Allocated fishing registration LT532 1919 Transferred to County Fishing Co. Ltd. 1927 Sold to T. Stephens, Aberdeen 1927 Allocated fishing registration A226 1940 Requisitioned by Admiralty for minesweeping 1940 Allocated pennant number FY1810 1946 Returned to owner 1947 In the ownership of Derry Trawling Co. Ltd. 1955 Sold for scrapping at Antwerp
Strathfinella LT63	Trawler GKGL 129348	192 74	113 x 22 x 12 Steel	Steam Triple 67hp Hall Russell	1910 Hall Russell Aberdeen	Built as A341 for Scottish owners 1919 Purchased by Jack Breach Ltd. 1924 Sold to A. Robertson 1924 Allocated fishing registration A63 1947 In the ownership of J. C. Robertson, Aberdeen 1955 In the ownership of Broomhill Fishing Co. Ltd. 1955 Sold for scrapping

Name Fishing Registration Port Registration	Vessel Type Call Sign RSS/ON	Gross Tonnage Net Tonnage	Dimensions (ft) Construction	Propulsion Unit(s) Make	Build Date Build Yard Build Location	History
Strathgeldie LT571	Trawler GQQL 129365	192 74	113 x 22 x 12 Steel	Steam Triple 67hp Hall Russell	1911 Hall Russell Aberdeen	Built as A399 for Scottish owners 1914 Requisitioned by Admiralty 1919 Returned to owners 1919 Sold to Frederick Spashett 1919 Transferred to County Fishing Co. Ltd. 1927 Sold to D. Dryburgh 1927 Allocated fishing registration GN99 1947 In the ownership of W. Brebner, Aberdeen & others 1960 Sold for scrapping
Strathlossie LT511	Trawler GRRX 129339	192 74	113 x 22 x 12 Steel	Steam Triple 67hp Hall Russell	1910 Hall Russell Aberdeen	Built as A316 for Scottish owners 1914 Requisitioned by Admiralty 1919 Returned to owners 1919 Sold to Frederick Spashett 1919 Transferred to Resolute Fishing Co. Ltd. 1923 Sold to J. Walker, Aberdeen 1923 Allocated fishing registration A952 1947 In the ownership of Faithlie Fishing Co. Ltd.
Strive LT133	Drifter/ Trawler GYPR 132378	102 46	89 x 19 x 9 Steel	Steam Triple 35hp Crabtree	1912 Crabtree Gt. Yarmouth	Built as YH665 Fred Salmon for J. T. & F. J. Salmon 1913 Transferred to J. T. Salmon 1921 Sold to D. & J. Windram, Eyemouth 1921 Became BK417 Ocean Plough in February 1930 Sold to Jack Breach Ltd. 1930 Became LT133 Strive 1939 In the ownership of Explorator Ltd. 1947 In the ownership of County Fishing Co. Ltd. 1953 Sold for scrapping during May
Suffolk Blazer London	Supply Ship GOYN 307975	854 387	188 x 38 x 11 Steel	Diesel 2 x 8cyl 1600hp Blackstone	1965 Hall Russell Aberdeen	Built as Lady Alison for International Offshore, London 1974 Sold to Sea Services Shipping Ltd. 1974 Renamed Aberdeen Blazer 1976 Owner taken over by Small & Co. (Lowestoft) Ltd. 1976 Renamed Suffolk Blazer 1987 Sold to Warbler Shipping Co. Ltd. 1987 Renamed Dawn Blazer 1994 Warbler Shipping and PE fleets merged 1994 Renamed Putford Blazer 1995 Sold and became Sea King 1995 Left Lowestoft on 27th October

| Name | Vessel Type | Gross Tonnage | Dimensions (ft) | Propulsion | Build Date | History |
| Fishing Registration | Call Sign | Net Tonnage | Construction | Unit(s) | Build Yard | |
Port Registration	RSS/ON			Make	Build Location	
Suffolk Challenger LT555 Lowestoft	Trawler GYMH 336021 A18990	255 91	125 x 26 x 13 Steel	Diesel 1 x 6cyl 1100hp Ruston	1968 Appledore SB Appledore	Built for Small & Co. (Lowestoft) Ltd. 1968 Launched on 18th March as Yard No. 55 1980 Converted for use as a SSV 1986 Sold to Anglo Spanish owners Elcander Ltd. 1986 Allocated fishing registration LT373 1986 Left Lowestoft on 24th December 1987 Renamed Jer Dos 1995 Reverted to original name
Suffolk Champion LT333	Stn. Trawler GBJW 376339	313 106	109 x 30 x 16 Steel	Diesel 1 x 12cyl 1200hp Blackstone	1980 Richards Gt. Yarmouth Yard No. 546	Built for Small & Co. (Lowestoft) Ltd. 1982 Landings for year totalled £303,431 1984 Fishing registration cancelled 1984 Converted for use as a SSV in May 1989 Owners interests taken over by Britannia Marine 1989 Renamed Britannia Champion 1994 Sold to Icelandic owners 1994 Became Leifur Eiriksson (of Reykjavik) 1996 Became Skude Pioneer (of Skudeneshavn)
Suffolk Chieftain LT556	Trawler GYMK 336027 A18989	255 91	125 x 26 x 13 Steel	Diesel 1 x 6cyl 1100hp Ruston	1968 Appledore SB Appledore	Built for Small & Co. (Lowestoft) Ltd. 1968 Arrived at Lowestoft on 24th June 1968 Left 28th June on first trip under Skipper J. Soanes 1980 Converted for use as a SSV 1986 Sold to Anglo Spanish owners Seaflow Ltd 1986 Allocated fishing registration LT372 1986 Left Lowestoft in September
Suffolk Conquest LT317 Lowestoft	Stn. Trawler GQHE 362274	392 134	120 x 30 x 13 Steel	Diesel 2 x 8cyl 2000hp Blackstone	1974 Cubow Woolwich	Built for Small & Co. (Lowestoft) Ltd. 1977 Working off Bombay on survey work 1980 Fishing registration cancelled 1980 Converted for use as a SSV/Survey Vessel 1989 Owners interests taken over by Britannia Marine 1989 Renamed Britannia Conquest 2001 In use on SSV duties

Name Fishing Registration Port Registration	Vessel Type Call Sign RSS/ON	Gross Tonnage Net Tonnage	Dimensions (ft) Construction	Propulsion Unit(s) Make	Build Date Build Yard Build Location	History
Suffolk County LT1059	Drifter 125853	87 36	84 x 19 x 9 Wood	Steam Compound 20hp E & G	1907 Chambers Lowestoft	Built as Spearmint for Captain W. Lucas 1908 Renamed Suffolk County 1911 Transferred to County Fishing Co. Ltd. 1914 Sold to Scottish owners 1914 Allocated fishing registration KY6 1924 Sold to Scottish owners 1924 Allocated fishing registration FR30 1933 Sold for breaking up
Suffolk Craftsman LT422	Trawler MEFW 302105	202 66	107 x 23 x 10 Steel	Diesel 1 x 6cyl 550hp Ruston	1961 Richards Lowestoft Yard No. 462	Built for Small & Co. (Lowestoft) Ltd. 1974 Sold to Putford Enterprises Ltd. 1975 Renamed Winkleigh in January 1981 Fishing registration cancelled 1981 Converted for use as a SSV
Suffolk Craftsman LT372	Trawler MEHZ 303280	283 88	124 x 25 x 12 Steel	Diesel 1 x 12cyl 790hp Brons	1961 Cochrane Selby	Built as GY672 Priscillian for Dominion S. F. Co. Ltd. 1976 Sold to Small & Co. (Lowestoft) Ltd. 1977 Became LT372 Suffolk Craftsman 1980 Sold to Greek owner John Xiros and renamed Ion 1984 Sold for scrapping
Suffolk Crusader LT557 Lowestoft	Trawler GYMG 336030 A18984	255 91	125 x 26 x 13 Steel	Diesel 1 x 6cyl 1100hp Ruston	1968 Appledore SB Appledore	Built for Small & Co. (Lowestoft) Ltd. 1980 Converted for use as a SSV 1987 Sold to Anglo Spanish owners 1987 Allocated fishing registration LT350 1991 Renamed Regina 1994 Renamed North Sea Coast 1997 Allocated fishing registration AR350
Suffolk Endeavour LT789	Trawler GYBT 309517 A18991	255 91	125 x 26 x 13 Steel	Diesel 1 x 6cyl 1100hp Ruston	1968 Appledore SB Appledore	Built for Kittiwake Ltd. 1967 Launched on 16th Nov. by Mrs. D. F. Cartwright 1968 Arrived at Lowestoft on 29th January 1968 Left on first trip 1st Feb. under Skipper T. Reynolds 1976 Fishing registration cancelled 1976 Converted for use as a Support/Survey/SSV 1977 Transferred to Small & Co. (Lowestoft) Ltd. 1977 Allocated fishing registration LT264 1980 Fully converted for use as a SSV 1987 Sold to Anglo Spanish owners 1987 Allocated fishing registration LT374 1987 Left Lowestoft on 18th February

Name Fishing Registration Port Registration	Vessel Type Call Sign RSS/ON	Gross Tonnage Net Tonnage	Dimensions (ft) Construction	Propulsion Unit(s) Make	Build Date Build Yard Build Location	History
Suffolk Enterprise LT492	Trawler MIXV 181390	245 81	115 x 26 x 10 Steel	Diesel 1 x 6cyl 760hp Mirrlees	1957 Vosper Portsmouth	Built as GY421 Boston Vanguard for the St. Andrews Steam Fishing Co. Ltd 1962 Sold to Vve Bon & Cie, La Rochelle 1962 Became LR5003 Imprevu 1965 Sold to Kittiwake Ltd. 1965 Arrived at Lowestoft on 15th November as Imprevu 1965 Became LT492 Suffolk Enterprise 1973 Transferred to Small & Co. (Lowestoft) Ltd. 1974 Sold to Claridge Trawlers Ltd. 1975 Renamed St. James during February 1980 Converted for use as a SSV 1980 Fishing registration cancelled 1986 Sold for scrapping in July 1986 Left Lowestoft on 21st August for the shipbreakers
Suffolk Enterprise London	Supply Ship 	677 247	158 x 38 x 15 Steel	Diesel 2 x 8cyl 1600hp Blackstone	1966 Bolsen Poole	Built as Lady Brigid for P & O Offshore Services 1974 Sold to Sea Service Shipping Ltd. 1974 Became Lowland Blazer 1976 Owner taken over by Small & Co. (Lowestoft) Ltd. 1976 Became Suffolk Enterprise 1983 Sold to Sea Trec Enterprises Inc. 1984 In use as a offshore buoy maintenance ship
Suffolk Harvester LT175 Lowestoft	Stn. Trawler GQUX 359295	422 134	130 x 29 x 13 Steel	Diesel 2 x 8cyl 2000hp Blackstone	1972 Cubow Woolwich	Built for Small & Co. (Lowestoft) Ltd 1977 Allocated fishing registration LT515 1978 Fishing registration cancelled 1978 Chartered to MOD (Navy) 1978 Became HMS Venturer M08 1978 Allocated to South Wales Division RNR 1983 Returned to owner 1984 Converted for use as a SSV 1989 Owners interests taken over by Britannia Marine 1989 Renamed Britannia Harvester 2001 In use on SSV duties
Suffolk Kinsman LT397	Trawler GHDX 302386	202 66	107 x 23 x 11 Steel	Diesel 1 x 6cyl 550hp Ruston	1960 Richards Lowestoft Yard No. 457	Built for Small & Co. (Lowestoft) Ltd. 1974 Sold to BDSF in September 1974 Renamed Boston Kinsman 1978 Sold to Sicily and became Nuovo Diddoro

Name	Vessel Type	Gross Tonnage	Dimensions (ft)	Propulsion	Build Date	History
Fishing Registration	Call Sign	Net Tonnage	Construction	Unit(s)	Build Yard	
Port Registration	RSS/ON			Make	Build Location	

Suffolk Kinsman	Tug/	708	177 x 38 x 15	Diesel	1969	Built as Cook Shore (of Sydney) for Osmarine Pty Ltd.
	Supply Ship	322	Steel	2 x 12cyl	Adelaide SC	1978 Purchased by Small & Co. (Lowestoft) Ltd.
London	GUHV			1200hp	Adelaide	1978 Renamed Suffolk Kinsman
	332997			Blackstone		1986 Sold to Eurosalve Ltd., Hastings
						1986 Renamed Eurosalve II
						1990 Sold to Western Ocean Towage Co. Ltd.
						1990 Renamed Cornishman
						1991 Sold to Putford Enterprises Ltd.
						1991 Arrived at Lowestoft on 3rd May
						1991 Renamed Putford Snipe
						1991 Converted for use as a SSV
						1995 Sold and became Stella Dena
Suffolk Maid	Trawler	130	91 x 22 x 11	Diesel	1957	Built for Small & Co. (Lowestoft) Ltd.
LT295	MXKS	54	Steel	1 x 6cyl	Richards	1970 Sold to J. M. Wilson of Anstruther
Lowestoft	187015			360hp	Lowestoft	1970 Became KY338 Anna Christina
				Ruston	Yard No. 435	1980 Sold to Putford Enterprises Ltd.
						1980 Fishing registration cancelled
						1980 Fully converted for use as a SSV
						1984 Renamed Putford Falcon, registered at Kirkcaldy
						1991 Advertised for sale at £84,000
						1992 Sold and later became Jolly Roger I
						1992 Left Lowestoft on 8th January
Suffolk Maid	Trawler	302	124 x 25 x 12	Diesel	1961	Built as GY673 Tiberian for Sir Thomas Robinson & Son
LT349	MEHY	95	Steel	1 x 12cyl	Cochrane	1976 Sold to Colne Fishing Co. Ltd.
	303281			790hp	Selby	1976 Arrived at Lowestoft on 29th October
				Brons		1976 Allocated fishing registration LT273
						1977 Converted for use as a SSV
						1977 Transferred to Dagon Fishing Co. Ltd.
						1978 Purchased by Small & Co. (Lowestoft) Ltd.
						1978 Became LT349 Suffolk Maid
						1981 Sold to J. Elinour for use as a Caribbean trader
						1984 In November during Hurricane "Klaus" broke away from her moorings
						1984 Grounded off Frederiksted, St. Croix
						1985 Attempts made to free the vessel's remains.
						1986 In January refloated and then sunk in Butler Bay to form an artificial reef

Name / Fishing Registration / Port Registration	Vessel Type / Call Sign / RSS/ON	Gross Tonnage / Net Tonnage	Dimensions (ft) / Construction	Propulsion Unit(s) / Make	Build Date / Build Yard / Build Location	History
Suffolk Mariner LT378	Trawler GHKB 302396	202 66	107 x 23 x 11 Steel	Diesel 1 x 6cyl 550hp Ruston	1961 Richards Lowestoft Yard No. 460	Built for Small & Co. (Lowestoft) Ltd. 1974 Sold to Pentode Ltd. (BDSF) 1974 Renamed Boston Mariner 1980 Sold to S. & C. Shooter of Durban 1981 Renamed Mariner 1983 Transferred to Mariner Trawling (Pty) Ltd.
Suffolk Mariner Aberdeen	Supply Ship GHGS 701187	1532 647	197 x 48 x 21 Steel	Diesel 3 x 8cyl 4780hp Blackstone	1986 Richards Lowestoft Yard No. 572	Built for Small & Co. (Lowestoft) Ltd 1989 Owners interests taken over by Britannia Marine 1997 Purchased by Trico Shipping AS 1997 Renamed Northern Marine
Suffolk Monarch LT170 Lowestoft	Stn. Trawler GRIB 362266	433 134	130 x 29 x 13 Steel	Diesel 2 x 8cyl 2000hp Blackstone	1973 Cubow Woolwich	Built for Small & Co. (Lowestoft) Ltd 1978 Fishing registration cancelled 1978 Chartered by the MOD (Navy) 1978 Became HMS St. Davids M07 1978 Allocated to Severn Division RNR 1983 Returned to owner 1984 Converted for use as a SSV 1989 Owners interests taken over by Britannia Marine 1989 Renamed Britannia Monarch 2001 In use on SSV duties
Suffolk Prince Aberdeen	Supply Ship/ Tug/Anchor Handling GCPD 377936	985 402	197 x 43 x 17 Steel	Diesel 2 x 6cyl 2112hp Blackstone	1982 Clelands Wallsend	Built for Small & Co. (Lowestoft) Ltd. 1989 Owners interests taken over by Britannia Marine 1990 Sold to Great Eastern Shipping Co., Bombay 1990 Renamed Malaviyn Seven 1996 Sold and became Oil Tempest
Suffolk Princess Aberdeen	Supply Ship/ Tug/ Anchor Handling GCPE 377939	985 401	197 x 43 x 17 Steel	Diesel 2 x 6cyl 2112hp Blackstone	1982 Clelands Wallsend	Built for Small & Co. (Lowestoft) Ltd. 1989 Owners interests taken over by Britannia Marine 1990 Sold to Great Eastern Shipping Co., Bombay 1990 Renamed Malaviyn Eight 1996 Sold and became Oil Typhoon

Name Fishing Registration Port Registration	Vessel Type Call Sign RSS/ON	Gross Tonnage Net Tonnage	Dimensions (ft) Construction	Propulsion Unit(s) Make	Build Date Build Yard Build Location	History
Suffolk Punch LT395	Trawler MEET 320400	202 66	107 x 23 x 11 Steel	Diesel 1 x 6cyl 550hp Ruston	1961 Richards Lowestoft Yard No. 461	Built for Small & Co. (Lowestoft) Ltd. 1974 Sold to Putford Enterprises Ltd. 1974 Renamed Hatherleigh 1983 Fishing registration cancelled 1983 Fully converted for use as a SSV 1993 Sold to Pindar plc, Scarborough 1993 Port registration changed 21st Sept. to Scarborough 1993 Converted for use as a hospitality/ MVS vessel 2001 Remains in service with Pindar plc/ MVS
Suffolk Sentinel LT348 Lowestoft	Trawler GXDH 309502 A18982	255 91	125 x 26 x 13 Steel	Diesel 1 x 6cyl 1100hp Ruston	1967 Appledore SB Appledore	Built as LT979 Constance Banks for EAI & CS 1967 Launched on 23rd May 1981 Landings for year totalled £297,851 1982 Made final landing in March 1982 Transferred to Small & Co. (Lowestoft) Ltd. 1982 Fishing registration cancelled 1982 Converted for use as a SSV 1982 Became Suffolk Sentinel 1986 Sold to Anglo Spanish owner Tankis Fisheries Ltd. 1986 Allocated fishing registration LT 348 1986 Left Lowestoft on 20th September 1986 Sold to Winleap Ltd. in November 1992 Renamed North Coast 1997 Allocated fishing registration AR96
Suffolk Supporter Aberdeen	Supply Ship LIPE	1969 845	219 x 52 x 23 Steel	Diesel 1 x 9cyl 5420hp Normo	1996 Soviknes Solik	Built for Suffolk Marine (Britannia Marine) 1997 Purchased by Trico Shipping AS 1997 Renamed Northern Supporter
Suffolk Venturer LT777	Trawler GXTA 309512	255 91	125 x 26 x 13 Steel	Diesel 1 x 6cyl 1100hp Ruston	1967 Appledore SB Appledore	Built for Smith & Co. (Lowestoft) Ltd. 1967 Launched on 22nd June as Yard No. 31 1967 Arrived at Lowestoft on 26th September 1967 Sailed 30th Sept. on first trip under "Jumbo" Fiske 1981 Landings for year totalled £266,628 1982 Converted for use as a SSV 1987 Sold to Anglo Spanish owners 1987 Allocated fishing registration LT349 1987 Left Lowestoft on 7th April 1994 Became AR95 South Coast

Name	Vessel Type	Gross Tonnage	Dimensions (ft)	Propulsion	Build Date	History
Fishing Registration	Call Sign	Net Tonnage	Construction	Unit(s)	Build Yard	
Port Registration	RSS/ON			Make	Build Location	

Suffolk Venturer
Supply Ship · 607 · 152 x 33 x 12 · Diesel · 1965
GJNC · 182 · Steel · 2 x 8cyl · Verolms
London · 713085 · 1700hp · Heusden · Kromhout

History:
Built as Lady Laura (of Rotterdam) for Offshore Marine
1974 Sold to Decca Navigation Ltd
1974 Renamed Decca Mariner (of Panama)
1980 Sold to Aventuris SA
1980 Renamed Bon Venture (of Panama)
1990 Purchased by Suffolk Marine (Britannia Marine)
1990 Arrived at Lowestoft on 12th June
1990 Converted for use as a SSV
1990 Renamed Suffolk Venturer (of London)
1991 Renamed Britannia Venturer
2001 Laid up at Lowestoft

Suffolk Warrior
Drifter/ · 147 · 94 x 22 x 10 · Diesel · 1960
LT671 · Trawler · 52 · Steel · 1 x 5cyl · Richards
MCUE · 377hp · Lowestoft
301535 · Ruston · Yard No. 456

History:
Built for Small & Co. (Lowestoft) Ltd.
1964 Prunier Trophy winner under Skipper Ernest Fiske
1969 Total loss on 15th February in the North Sea after a
    collision with the trawler KW81 Hendrika Johanna

Suffolk Warrior
Stn. Trawler · 392 · 130 x 29 x 15 · Diesel · 1973
LT171 · GREN · 134 · Steel · 2 x 8cyl · Cubow
Lowestoft · 359309 · 2000hp · Woolwich · Blackstone

History:
Built for Small & Co. (Lowestoft) Ltd.
1973 Landed record catch of £11,139 (Skipper D. Smith)
1974 In use on survey work
1977 Converted for use as a fire fighting/SSV
1989 Owners interests taken over by Britannia Marine
1989 Renamed Britannia Warrior
2001 In use on SSV duties

Sussex County
Drifter · 83 · 84 x 18 x 8 · Steam · 1908
LT63 · 40 · Steel · Compound · Cochrane
127599 · 31hp · Selby · Crabtree

History:
Built for W. Lucas
1908 Transferred to County Fishing Co. Ltd.
1914-18 Sold to Admiralty
1921 Sold back to County Fishing Co. Ltd.
1939 Requisitioned by Admiralty for auxiliary patrol use
1945 Returned to owner in April
1946 Sold to Norway
1946 Left Lowestoft on 29th July

Swiftwing
Drifter/ · 98 · 86 x 19 x 9 · Steam · 1912
LT675 · Trawler · 41 · Steel · Triple · Torry SB
GZPS · 34hp · Aberdeen
127358 · Abernethy

History:
Built as BF496 for Scottish owners
1920 Purchased by Jack Breach Ltd.
1946 Transferred to County Fishing Co. Ltd.
1947 In the ownership of Shoals Fishing Co. Ltd.
1949 Sold for scrapping at Oulton Broad

Name Fishing Registration Port Registration	Vessel Type Call Sign RSS/ON	Gross Tonnage Net Tonnage	Dimensions (ft) Construction	Propulsion Unit(s) Make	Build Date Build Yard Build Location	History
Swiftwing LT238	Drifter/ Trawler GYPP 145827	99 45	86 x 19 x 9 Steel	Diesel 1 x 4cyl 240hp Ruston	1925 Cochrane Selby	Built as steam drifter Sternus for Seagull Fishing Co. Ltd. 1954 Steam engine replaced by diesel 1954 Renamed Swiftwing 1964 Sold to Lola Fishing Co. Ltd., Hartlepool 1964 Registration changed to HL147 1970 Sold for scrapping
Taal Hina LT621	Drifter 140023	94 41	87 x 20 x 10 Wood	Steam Triple 46hp Cooper & Greig	1919 Stevenson & Asher Banff	Built as HMD Sunrise for Admiralty 1919 Became LT621 Sunrise 1920 Renamed Taal Hina 1923 Purchased by Resolute Fishing Co. Ltd., Lowestoft 1923 Renamed Scania 1926 Sold to J. Buchan, St. Combs 1926 Became FR190 Tillyduff 1939 Requisitioned by Admiralty for minesweeping 1939 Allocated pennant number FY939 1946 Returned to owner in August
Thankful LT1035	Drifter 124435	55 28	73 x 18 x 8 Wood	Steam Compound 15hp E & G	1907 Reynolds Oulton Broad	Built for Brauer & Betts Ltd., Lowestoft as motor drifter 1908 Transferred to H. J. Betts Ltd. 1908 60 ihp Brauer & Betts motor replaced by steam 1910 Sold to Eastern Drifters Ltd. 1918 Sold to Streanshalk Fishing Co. Ltd., Whitby 1918 Allocated fishing registration WY241 1920 Offered for sale during September at Ramsgate 1923 Sold to Ramsgate Legion Shipbreaking Co. Ltd. 1925 Passed to National Provincial & Union Bank of England 1925 Sold for breaking up
Three Kings LT517	Drifter/ Trawler GZPR 127357	98 41	86 x 18 x 9 Steel	Steam Triple 34hp Abernethy	1912 Torry SB Aberdeen	Built as BF495 for Scottish owners 1914-18 War Service 1920 Purchased by Jack Breach Ltd. 1939 Requisitioned by Admiralty for minesweeping 1939 Allocated pennant number FY918 1944 Returned to owner in September 1946 In the ownership of Shoals Fishing Co. Ltd. 1946 Registry closed 1950 Sold for scrapping

Name Fishing Registration Port Registration	Vessel Type Call Sign RSS/ON	Gross Tonnage Net Tonnage	Dimensions (ft) Construction	Propulsion Unit(s) Make	Build Date Build Yard Build Location	History
Thrifty LT152	Drifter/ Trawler GJZG 149228	145 68	99 x 20 x 10 Steel	Diesel 1 x 3cyl 300hp AKD	1916 Godreeders Leiderdorp	Built as steam powered IJM255 Baltic for Dutch owners 1919 Sold to Belgium owner and became Fernando 1928 Sold to Dutch owner and became IJM54 Limburgia 1929 Sold to S. Allerton, R. Read & Frederick Spashett 1929 Became LT152 Thrifty 1938 Transferred to S. Allerton and Frederick Spashett 1939 Transferred to Kittiwake Ltd. 1939 Requisitioned by Admiralty for minesweeping use 1939 Allocated pennant number FY1523 1945 Transferred to Small & Co. (Lowestoft) Ltd. 1946 Returned to owner in April 1946 Transferred to Kittiwake Ltd 1955 Steam engine replaced by diesel 1960 Sold to Alvis Trawlers Ltd., Fleetwood 1960 Allocated fishing registration FD201 1967 Alvis Trawlers Ltd. sold to Skipper Bert Andrews 1967 Renamed Catherine Shaun in March 1968 Transferred to ownership of WFA 1968 Offered for sale by WFA 1971 Sold for scrapping
Togo LT609	Drifter/ Trawler GJRN 120341	75 28	80 x 18 x 9 Steel	Steam Compound 28hp Crabtree	1905 Fellows Gt. Yarmouth	Built as YH477 for Fellows & Co. Ltd. 1906 Sold to Admiral Fishing Co. Ltd. 1906 Allocated fishing registration LT609 1920 Sold to Robert Balls 1920 Allocated fishing registration YH248 1935 Transferred to Ronald Balls, S. Tunbridge and Robert Randell in March 1935 Sold to A. Ling & S. Bird in July 1938 Allocated fishing registration LT69 1935 Steam engine replaced by 3cyl 200hp Mirrlees 1935 Transferred to Jubilee Fishing Co. Ltd. 1958 Sold to Colne Fishing Co. Ltd. 1964 Sold for scrapping 1964 Left for shipbreakers on 8th October towing the hulk of the trawler Tobago

Name	Vessel Type	Gross Tonnage	Dimensions (ft)	Propulsion	Build Date	History
Fishing Registration	Call Sign	Net Tonnage	Construction	Unit(s)	Build Yard	
Port Registration	RSS/ON			Make	Build Location	
Touchwood LT1150	Drifter 130050	84 37	83 x 18 x 9 Steel	Steam Compound 32hp Crabtree	1911 Crabtree Gt. Yarmouth	Built as Merry Spinner for V & B Stephens 1914 Sold to H. Baxter, Frederick Spashett, W.Catchpole 1914 Renamed Touchwood 1914 Requisition by Admiralty 1919 Returned to owners 1919 Transferred to Eastern Drifters Ltd. 1929 Transferred to Seagull Fishing Co. Ltd. 1930 Renamed Marinus 1939 Requisitioned by Admiralty for use as a barrage balloon vessel 1946 Returned to owner 1946 Sold to Norway for use as a trader 1946 Left Lowestoft during August towed by Sunnyside Girl
Trier LT158	Drifter/ Trawler GNDT 149231	136 61	100 x 20 x 10 Steel	Steam Triple 225hp Burgerhaut	1917 Godreeders Leiderdorp	Built as IJM258 Oceanic for Witte Ster 1919 Sold and became F595 Lizette Adolphine 1928 Sold to Limburgia and became IJM171 Zeelandia 1929 Sold to F. Spashett & S. Allerton 1929 Became LT158 Trier 1939 Transferred to Kittiwake Ltd. 1945 Transferred to Small & Co. (Lowestoft) Ltd. 1946 Transferred to Frederick Spashett 1947 Transferred to Trier Fishing Co. Ltd. 1954 Sold to W. James (Milford Haven) Ltd. 1956 Sold for scrapping
Tritonia LT188	Drifter/ Trawler GYWN 149246	115 52	92 x 20 x 9 Steel	Steam Triple 50hp Burrell	1930 Chambers Lowestoft	Built for Herring Fishing Co. Ltd. 1936 Sold to Sydney J. Tripp 1940 Requisitioned by the Admiralty for minesweeping 1940 Assigned pennant number FY973 1945 Sold to Vigilant Fishing Co. Ltd. 1946 Returned to owner in January by the Admiralty 1957 Sold to Mitchells Tritonia Ltd 1957/8 Steam engine replaced by 335hp Ruston diesel 1975 Sold to Colne Fishing Co. Ltd. in November 1976 Sold for scrapping to T. G. Darling, Oulton Broad

Name Fishing Registration Port Registration	Vessel Type Call Sign RSS/ON	Gross Tonnage Net Tonnage	Dimensions (ft) Construction	Propulsion Unit(s) Make	Build Date Build Yard Build Location	History
Two Boys LT1157	Drifter 132937	90 41	87 x 20 x 10 Wood	Steam Triple 25hp E & G	1911 Chambers Lowestoft	Built for G. Snowling 1914-18 War Service 1919 Sold to J. V. Breach 1921 Transferred to J. V. Breach and E.T.Capps 1921 Transferred to Kittiwake Ltd 1936 Sold for breaking up at Sunderland
United Boys LT53	Drifter/ Trawler GYDV 135063	95 40	86 x 19 x 9 Steel	Steam Triple 34hp Crabtree	1913 Crabtree Gt. Yarmouth	Built for J. T. Salmon as YH295 Girl Kathleen 1924 Collided in fog with Pevensey Castle on 9th June off Johnshaven. Pevensey Castle declared a total loss 1924 Sold to Kittiwake Ltd 1924 Became LT53 United Boys in September 1931 Transferred to J. V. Breach 1938 Transferred to Kittiwake Ltd. 1939 Requisitioned by Admiralty for minesweeping 1939 Allocated pennant number FY855 1945 Returned to owner in September 1946 Sold to Norway
United Friends LT55	Drifter 135736	91 40	84 x 19 x 10 Wood	Steam Compound 20hp E & G	1913 Chambers Lowestoft	Built as Star of Thule for Jas. Shearer, Whalsay 1923 Sold to Kittiwake Ltd 1923 Renamed United Friends 1939 Sold for breaking up in Holland 1941 Sold and fished for Dutch owners until 1946
Victoria LT1056	Drifter 124445	92 22	85 x 19 x 9 Steel	Steam Triple 25hp Shanks	1907 Montrose SB Montrose	Built for Britannia Fishing Co. Ltd 1914-19 War Service (Victoria II 1915-1919) 1925 Sold to Scottish owners 1925 Allocated fishing registration BCK117
W. F. Cockrell LT213	Trawler MLDQ 183969	96 40	81 x 21 x 9 Steel	Diesel 1 x 4cyl 231hp Ruston	1950 Richards Lowestoft Yard No. 400	Built for East Anglian Ice & Cold Storage Ltd. 1966 Transferred to Small & Co. (Lowestoft) Ltd. 1966 Sold to Mr. J. G. Segalla, Capetown 1966 Left Lowestoft on 14th September
West Anglia LT528	Drifter 129970	74 33	84 x 18 x 8 Wood	Steam Compound 29hp Crabtree	1910 Chambers Lowestoft	Built for Dreadnought Fishing Co. Ltd. 1914-18 War Service 1920 Transferred to Eastern Drifters Ltd. 1929 Transferred to Seagull Fishing Co. Ltd. 1936 Sold for breaking up

Name Fishing Registration Port Registration	Vessel Type Call Sign RSS/ON	Gross Tonnage Net Tonnage	Dimensions (ft) Construction	Propulsion Unit(s) Make	Build Date Build Yard Build Location	History
Willing Boys LT737	Drifter/ Trawler GZKL 149229	138 59	98 x 21 x 10 Steel	Steam Triple 280hp Crabtree	1930 Chambers Lowestoft	Built for Catchpole, Utting, Baxter, Dance & Co. Ltd. 1939 Requisitioned by the Admiralty for minesweeping 1939 Assigned pennant number FY947 1945 Sold to Pevensey Castle Ltd 1946 Returned to owner in August by the Admiralty 1952 Last year of herring fishing 1953 Sold to W. H. Kerr (Ship Chandlers) Ltd. 1957 Steam engine replaced with 440hp Crossley diesel 1974 Sold to Brigg Trawling Co. Ltd., Milford Haven 1977 Sold for scrapping to T. W. Ward Ltd., Briton Ferry
Wishful LT661	Drifter 129985	83 34	83 x 19 x 9 Steel	Steam Compound 32hp Crabtree	1910 Cochrane Selby	Built for Eastern Drifters Ltd. 1914-19 War Service 1919 Returned to owner in July 1919 Sold and allocated fishing registration WY247 1921 Lost after a collision on 10th February
Young Dawn LT1294	Drifter 139777	86 36	88 x 19 x 9 Wood	Steam Triple 38hp Lewis	1916 Stephen Banff	Built as A665 for Scottish owners 1916-19 Requisitioned by Admiralty 1919 Returned to owner 1923 Sold to Frederick Spashett 1923 Sold to P. G. Warman 1927 Sold to Northern Fishing Co. Ltd. 1927 Allocated fishing registration PD178
Young Duke LT387	Drifter/ Trawler GRFS 183995	115 46	88 x 21 x 11 Steel	Diesel 1 x 5cyl 300hp Ruston	1953 Richards Lowestoft Yard No. 417	Built for Small & Co. (Lowestoft) Ltd. 1966 Whaleback fitted in December 1967 Sold to Marinex Gravel Ltd. in February 1967 Fishing registration cancelled on 11th April. 1967 Registered in London 1969 Sold to James Corson 1969 Became KY377 Spes Aurea 1973 Sold to Putford Enterprises Ltd. 1977 Fully converted for use as a SSV 1984 Renamed Southleigh 1987 Sold to Eurosalve Ltd. of Folkestone 1987 Converted for use as a diving support vessel 1987 Renamed Eurodive 1

Name Fishing Registration Port Registration	Vessel Type Call Sign RSS/ON	Gross Tonnage Net Tonnage	Dimensions(ft) Construction	Propulsion Unit(s) Make	Build Date Build Yard Build Location	History
Young Elizabeth LT375	Drifter/ Trawler GQZC 183993	115 46	88 x 21 x 11 Steel	Diesel 1 x 5cyl 300hp Ruston	1953 Richards Lowestoft Yard No. 416	Built for Small & Co. (Lowestoft) Ltd. 1966 Whaleback fitted in December 1968 In use on SSV work during January 1968 Sold to Offshore Oil Rig Services Ltd. 1968 Fishing registration cancelled in April 1968 In use on diving and research work 1976 Sold to Star Offshore Services Ltd. 1977 Converted for use as a SSV 1983 Sold to Putford Enterprises Ltd. 1984 Consideration given to rename Putford Hawk 1987 Sold to Vyvyan Rayner 1988 Registered as a yacht 2001 In use as a houseboat
Zealot LT1104	Drifter 127583	59 34	76 x 18 x 8 Wood	Steam Compound 20hp E & G	1907 Chambers Lowestoft	Built for F. J. Offord 1914 Sold to Catchpole, Gouldby and Hutchings 1918 Transferred to Brown and Hutchings 1921 Transferred to Laura Brown 1922 Sold to County Fishing Co. Ltd 1933 Sold to J. R. Foulkes, Bursledon. Left on river bank until 1955

LT1104 Zealot entering Lowestoft harbour
on the 20th April 1927.

Colour photographs of Small & Co. drifters displaying the Company colour scheme are quite rare. However, it is seen in these views of the following vessels.

Top Left - The steam drifter/trawler *LT133 Strive,* the second vessel from the camera. *Strive* was sold for scrapping in 1953.

Top Right - The diesel powered drifter/trawler *LT138 Frederick Spashett.* She was built in 1949 and sold in 1965.

Bottom Left - The last drifter/trawler built for Small & Co. was *LT671 Suffolk Warrior.* Completed in 1960 by Richards, she was lost following a collision in 1969.
This vessel was the first of two to be named *Suffolk Warrior*.

The very last fishing vessel built for the Company was the stern trawler *LT333 Suffolk Champion*. She was built in 1980 at the Yarmouth yard of Richards (Shipbuilders) Ltd. *Suffolk Champion* was later used on offshore support work, and was sold in 1989.

An early addition to the offshore oil and gas industry support fleet was the *Suffolk Blazer*. She was purchased in 1976 as the *Aberdeen Blazer*, having been built in 1965 at Aberdeen as *Lady Alison. Suffolk Blazer* was sold in 1987 and became *Dawn Blazer.*

She is seen at Richards (Shipbuilders) Ltd., Lowestoft yard. At the time of writing, outline planning permission has been granted by Waveney District Council for this historic maritime site to be redeveloped as a retail, business and leisure park. On the right can be seen the well known canning factory of the Cooperative Wholesale Society. This has now been demolished and the vacant site is scheduled to be used as an another business park.

With a new fishing registration of *LT349*, the safety standby vessel and former trawler *Suffolk Venturer* is ready to leave Lowestoft for the last time. She no longer carries the well known houseflag of Small & Co., and was set to return to fishing under Anglo Spanish ownership. As a Company trawler, *Suffolk Venturer* carried the fishing registration *LT777*.

After a few years involvement in the offshore oil and gas industry, Small & Co. had a number of offshore support vessels built for their fleet. The Aberdeen registered *Suffolk Princess* was one of a pair built in 1982.

A great day in 1986 at the shipyard of
Richards Shipbuilders in Lowestoft,
as the supply ship *Suffolk Mariner* is
prepared for her launching.
She was the second *Suffolk Mariner*
built for Small & Co. fleet. Both were
built by Richards, the first being a
trawler, which was sold during 1974.

A sign of changing times for the Company is indicated
here by the appearance of the safety standby vessel
Suffolk Venturer. Although flying the Small & Co.
houseflag, just visible on the exhaust uptake is the
emblem of Britannia Marine, her new owners. The
Suffolk Venturer, built as the supply ship *Lady Laura*
in 1965, and second vessel to carry that name, was later
renamed *Britannia Venturer*.
The first *Suffolk Venturer* was a trawler sold to Anglo
Spanish interests in 1987.

FLEET LOG

This lists, in alphabetical order, vessels associated with Small & Co. (Lowestoft) Ltd, the Spashett family, Suffolk Marine, and other associated owners. Included is the vessel name, other known previous names, and the period when she was in the fleet. It does not include chartered or managed vessels, and should not be consider as being conclusive.

Name	Previous Names	In Fleet	Name	Previous Names	In Fleet	Name	Previous Names	Period In
Acceptable		1924-1953	Fleurbaix	HMD Scud	1919-1939	Mary Heeley	Edward P. Wills	1949-1950
Amalia		1930-1946	Formidable		1917-1946	Mascot		1918-1927
Annrobin		1955-1968	Fort Albert		1918-1922	Meg		1919-1936
Ascona		1929-1953	Frederick Spashett		1949-1965	Nell Morgan		1899-1901
B. R. Banks		1951-1966	Fume	HMD Fume	1919-1930	Nelson		1906-1920
Barkis		1972-1976	George Spashett		1950-1965	Netsukis		1913-1947
Ben & Lucy		1925-1946	Gervais Rentoul		1920-1952	Neves		1945-1955
Ben Iver		1920-1923	Girl Gladys		1919-1947	Nil Desperandum		1908-1936
Boy Alan		1919-1941	Girls Friend		1906-1916	Norfolk County		1908-1946
Boy Nat	Hilda and Ernest	1919-1920	Go Ahead	HMD Volume	1919-1940	Norfolk Yeoman		1955-1968
		1924-1924	Golden Harvest		1939-1947	Ocean Crest		1963-1967
Boy Phillip		1930-1947	Good Hope		1907-1911	Ocean Dawn		1963-1969
Boy Roy		1917-1940	Green Dolphin	MMS112	1947-1949	Ocean Starlight		1963-1967
Boy Scout		1929-1944	Half Moon		1919-1936	Ocean Sunlight		1963-1967
Boys Friend	Martina		Happy Returns		1900-1920	Ocean Surf		1963-1969
	Annie	1936-1955	Harnser	HMD Windhowl	1919-1939	Ocean Trust		1963-1969
Byng	HMD Elephanta	1920-1931	Harold Cartwright		1950-1966	Olivae	Dorothy F	1924-1956
Cape Colony		1908-1913	Henrietta Spashett		1950-1966	Patria	Atlantic	
Capetown		1908-1915	Herring Searcher		1947-1954		Irma	1930-1954
Clansman	Ethel	1921-1926	John Alfred		1919-1927	Pevensey Castle		1917-1924
Colonial		1908-1927	John Alfred	Pleasants	1927-1946	Ploughboy		1919-1947
Constance Banks		1967-1982	John and Sarah		1901-1911	Plumer	HMD Windwail	1920-1947
Craske	Veracite		Kent County		1911-1916	Present Help		1911-1953
	Waterboat No.9	1949-1989	Kent County		1929-1932	Realise		1925-1932
Devon County	Scadaun	1912-1941	Kiddaw	Ruler of the Sea	1909-1951	Reality		1920-1932
Dewey		1908-1914	Lanner		1919-1947	Remembrance		1917-1919
Dick Whittington		1913-1950	Lavinia L		1924-1941	Resolute		1919-1919
Dick Whittington		1955-1968	Leonard Cockrell		1958-1971	Retriever		1930-1930
Dorienta	Happy Days	1936-1948	Linsdell		1914-1914	Reunited	George Hay	1929-1938
Drake	HMD Drake	1907-1914	Loch Broom		1919-1923	Reverberation		1919-1947
Eager		1933-1945	Loch Eriboll		1919-1921	Reward		1917-1929
East Anglia		1909-1915	London County		1909-1919	Rising Sun		1899-1900
Eileen Emma		1919-1946	Lurline		1895-1903	Rissa	Thomas Beeching	1924-1925
Emerald		1904-1906	Madame Prunier	Equity I	1952-1959	Rodney		1907-1923
Enterprise		1906-1916	Majesty		1908-1926	Rooke		1908-1916
Ethel Mary		1957-1969	Margaret Christina		1960-1970	Roy Stevens		1961-1974
Evening Primrose		1930-1947	Margaret Hide		1920-1955	Sarah Hide		1937-1955
Expectant		1920-1939	Marinus		1925-1929	Sarah Marian		1917-1920
Explorator		1919-1925	Marinus	Touchwood		Scania	Taal Hina	
Feasible		1930-1946		Merry Spinner	1930-1946		Sunrise	
Fellowship	Neves	1955-1961	Mary Bruce	Penicles	1948-1953		HMD Sunrise	1923-1926

112

Name	Previous Names	In Fleet	Name	Previous Names	In Fleet	Name	Previous Names	In Fleet
Scarborough		1918-1918	Suffolk Enterprise	Lady Brigid		Thankful		1910-1918
Score Head	Retriever	1930-1946		Lowland Blazer	1976-1983	Three Kings		1920-1950
Searcher		1915-1937	Suffolk Harvester		1972-1989	Thrifty	Limburgia	
Shipmates		1911-1940	Suffolk Kinsman		1960-1974		Baltic	
Silver Spray		1900-1901	Suffolk Kinsman	Cook Shore	1978-1986		Ferando	1929-1960
Skimmer of the Sea		1898-1899	Suffolk Maid		1957-1970	Togo		1906-1920
Sternus		1925-1950	Suffolk Maid	Tiberian	1978-1981	Touchwood	Merry Spinner	1914-1930
		1954-1954	Suffolk Mariner		1986-1989	Trier	Oceanic	
Strathderry		1919-1927	Suffolk Mariner		1961-1974		Lizette Adolphine	
Strathfinella		1919-1924	Suffolk Monarch		1973-1989		Zeelandia	1929-1954
Strathgeldie		1919-1927	Suffolk Prince		1982-1989	Tritonia		1945-1957
Strathlossie		1919-1923	Suffolk Princess		1982-1989	Two Boys		1919-1936
Strive	Fred Salmon		Suffolk Punch		1961-1974	United Boys	Girl Kathleen	1924-1946
	Ocean Plough	1930-1953	Suffolk Sentinel	Constance Banks	1982-1986	United Friends	Star of Thule	1923-1939
Suffolk Blazer	Lady Alison		Suffolk Supporter		1996-1997	Victoria		1907-1925
	Aberdeen Blazer	1976-1987	Suffolk Venturer		1967-1987	W. F. Cockrell		1950-1966
Suffolk Challenger		1968-1986	Suffolk Venturer	Lady Laura		West Anglia		1910-1936
Suffolk Champion		1980-1989		Decca Mariner		Willing Boys		1930-1952
Suffolk Chieftain		1968-1986		Bon Venture	1990-1990	Wishful		1910-1919
Suffolk Conquest		1974-1989	Suffolk Warrior		1960-1969	Young Dawn		1923-1923
Suffolk County	Spearmint	1911-1914	Suffolk Warrior		1973-1989	Young Duke		1953-1967
Suffolk Craftsman		1961-1974	Sussex County		1908-1914	Young Elizabeth		1953-1968
Suffolk Craftsman		1976-1980			1918-1946	Zealot		1907-1933
Suffolk Crusader		1968-1987	Swiftwing		1920-1949			
Suffolk Endeavour		1968-1987	Swiftwing	Sternus	1954-1964			
Suffolk Enterprise	Boston Vanguard		Taal Hina	HMD Sunrise				
	Imprevu	1965-1974		Sunrise	1923-1923			

A classic view of the 1961 built trawler *LT271 Roy Stevens* heading for sea.

This vessel was named after Mr. Roy Stevens, who in his early 40s, was tragically drowned under ice on the River Waveney, whilst attempting to save his dog.

Mr. Stevens, was the assistant manager of Explorator Ltd., and one of the leading figures in the local fishing industry at the time.

The *Roy Stevens* was registered in the ownership of Explorator Ltd.

Left - *Suffolk Endeavour,* one of the much
          admired trawlers built in Appledore
          seen after her full conversion for use
          as an offshore standby safety vessel.

Below - Shortly before her sale to Dutch
          interests and subsequent loss with all
          hands in 1967, *LT464 Ocean
          Sunlight* heads for the fishing
          grounds rigged for trawling.

LT151 BOYS FRIEND AND LT178 PATRIA FRESHLY PAINTED UP IN THE TRAWL DOCK DURING THE LATE 1930S. BOTH VESSELS WERE OWNED BY SUBSIDIARIES OF SMALL & CO. AND BUILT IN HOLLAND.

SELECT BIBLIOGRAPHY

Down The Harbour 1955-1995 by Malcolm White (White-1998)
40 years of fishing vessels, owners, the harbour and shipyards at Lowestoft

A Century of Fishing by Malcolm White (White-1999)
Fishing from Great Yarmouth and Lowestoft 1899-1999

Fishing with Diversity by Malcolm White (White-2000)
A portrait of the Colne Group of Lowestoft

Fishing News Various Editions (EMAP)
Olsen's Fisherman's Nautical Almanack Various (Dennis)
Lloyds Register of Shipping Various Editions (Lloyds)

PLRS Newsletters and Documents Various (PLRS)
Mercantile Navy List Various Editions (HMSO)
Maritime Directories Various Editions (HMSO)

ABC British Trawlers by Le Fleming (Ian Allan)

VESSEL PHOTOGRAPHIC INDEX

BACK COVER PHOTOGRAPHS

Left - Built by Richards (Shipbuilders) Ltd. in 1986 at their Lowestoft yard, *Suffolk Mariner* was included in the sale of the assets of Suffolk Marine to Britannia Marine in 1989. She was sold on in 1997 and renamed *Northern Mariner*. The newly completed *Suffolk Mariner* is seen here off Lowestoft.

Right - Representing the wide spectrum of business interests of Small & Co. (Lowestoft) Ltd. is this fine view of a Craske (Petroleum) Ltd. road tanker. The location is their Oulton Broad depot, which was located adjacent to Lake Lothing. The depot was sold and is now used for storage of surplus and scrap materials.

Still visible in 2001, a sign at the former premises of William Overy & Son.